Heart For God

Bob Sears

Heart For God
Bob Sears

Unless otherwise indicated, Scripture quotations are taken from The Holy Bible, *New International Version®, NIV®*. Copyright ©1973, 1978, 1984, 2011 by Biblica, Inc.® Used by permission. All rights reserved worldwide.

Scripture quotations marked NLT are taken from the *Holy Bible*, New Living Translation, copyright ©1996, 2004, 2015 by Tyndale House Foundation. Used by permission of Tyndale House Publishers, Carol Stream, Illiniois 60188. All rights reserved.

ISBN: 979-8-9944914-0-9

Please direct any comments or questions to the author at:
bobasears@gmail.com
(714) 612-0941

Table of Contents

ACKNOWLEDGMENTS

We don't know what we don't know; that's what friends are for. I'm deeply grateful to several of mine whose insights and suggestions made this book importantly better than it would have been without them: Katie Smylie, Dr. Jon Lunde, Lori Ann Bach, Gary Bostrom, Don Flecky, and Graig Oba. Angeli Takahashi, you are a skillful and gracious artist. Thank you for such an attractive product! And Leslie, you <u>always</u> do amazing work! I wonder if there's anything you can't create. Love you, Sis.

APPRECIATION

I wish I'd been able to figure out how to make this project less "costly" for my wife, Caroline. It took way longer than either of us expected, and I wasn't very attentive or spontaneous during much of that time. Still, she did a wonderful job of remaining patient, listening, encouraging me to continue and praying all the while. I'm so grateful to you, Sweetheart, for all your understanding and support. You are God's precious gift and my best friend.

DEDICATION

To the One who plucked me out of the fire so many years ago. Life with you has been more exhilarating, meaningful, purposeful, stable, fun and better than I could ever have hoped. Just as you promised. Earth has nothing I desire more than you. My flesh and my heart may fail, but you are the strength of my heart and my portion forever.

PREFACE

I learned almost nothing about God during my first 18 years. My parents were low-key atheists, so we never talked about faith or religion. Not once did we go to church. Mom adopted the notion of a Higher Power when she joined Alcoholics Anonymous in my senior year of high school, but she was clear that wasn't the same thing as a Bible-like God. Dad was simply uninterested and pragmatic about life. Neither of them ever changed their minds.

But *I* did after a powerful, unsought encounter with God soon after my 19th birthday. A friend had suggested on a lonesome Saturday night that we might be able to meet some girls if we visited the church he used to attend. So the next morning we went and we did.

Two young ladies there told us we should return that evening if we wanted to go out, so we did that too. But as we dutifully sat through the sermon, I became acutely aware that God was present and something was desperately wrong with me. If you knew the kind of person I had become by then, you would understand. The encounter broke my heart, and I responded tearfully and sincerely to the pastor's invitation to receive God's forgiveness. That night I began life over as a follower of Jesus. By the time I finished praying about that with a few people, the girls had left and my friend was disappointed. But I knew for certain that I was forgiven and something new had come to life in me.

I had no clue what to do next. I still loved using illicit drugs, got arrested for it (again) and spent a few enlightening months in jail. While there I prayed a little and read the Bible some. A local, part-time pastor visited once each week and encouraged me. Once released I started attending a lively church with a bunch of people my age who were excited about their faith. It was a great place to make a different kind of friends and begin to learn.

If you had asked me then what God was up to in my life, I probably would've answered that He just wanted me to obey his commandments and try to convert unbelievers. But I wasn't very good at either. I needed some ongoing, systematic, personalized guidance from someone more knowledgeable and mature, but nobody volunteered. So I wound up acquiring several unfortunate misunderstandings that stifled my joy and stunted my growth. I also remained oblivious to a few deeply-rooted flaws in my character which later led to some devastating failures.

Over the next 35 years I graduated from a great Bible college and seminary, became an associate pastor in a couple of good churches and served as a local missionary in the recovery community. I taught countless Bible studies and explored scores of topics designed to help Christians grow. But it took me way too long to understand the Bible's big picture and the few essential things that God cares about most. That appears to be a common experience. Many Christians shuffle along for years after their conversion with an incomplete or superficial understanding of what God has in mind and what it takes to follow Jesus.

Part of the problem is that the Bible is big and filled with so many stories, truths and instructions that we can easily lose the forest for the trees. It is a daunting collection of 66 ancient books written in three languages by 40+ authors over a period of 1500 years.

But it is also a single, unfolding story from beginning to end about God's eternal plan to surround Himself with a joyful family of people who freely respond to his love for them by loving him in return. That is the desire and promise he reiterates every time he's quoted as saying: "I will be your God and you will be my people."[1] How to get all-the-way-in on that is what this book is about.

PLEASE TAKE TO HEART these few comments and suggestions as you begin:

1. This material is meant to be used as a workbook and not merely read. Take your time. Your goal should be to absorb, not to finish.

2. If you decide to go through this on your own, please prayerfully think-through and write-out your answers to its many questions. They have been carefully crafted to make them personal, and they are an essential part of learning this material.

3. When some "POSSIBLE ANSWERS" are provided for you in response to a question in the text, try not to read them until you write your own. Then mark the ones you like.

4. While you read, add your own underlines, highlights, circles, arrows, question marks, comments, etc. so you'll be able to spot and discuss them easily later on.

5. You will get MUCH more out of this by doing it with others. Perhaps you could be the facilitator or, if you're further along, a mentor to the others. Far too few believers get adequately trained in how to live all of life as Jesus's "disciples" (student-apprentices), though He explicitly instructed us to make sure all of them do (Matthew 28:18-19). Just have the group agree to read a specified portion and answer all the questions (in writing) on their own, then meet to discuss everyone's findings. Once you finish the whole book you'll hopefully be ready to go through it again with someone else.

6. If you are in a group, you'll need to decide a couple of things in advance:

    •   Are you going to follow the recommendations I make on the right side of each page number in the Table of Contents regarding how much material each of your Study Sessions "should" cover? That breakdown is designed for groups that want to work through two full Sections every ten weeks. But choose whatever pace best suits you.

    •   How will you help people catch-up when they miss a session?

7. Feel free to call or write me if you'd like to talk. Or let's meet up. I live in Fullerton, California, with no plans to move until heaven.

    •   (714) 612-0941, bobasears@gmail.com

---

[1] This is repeated in a similar form many, many times throughout the Bible and is an obvious emphasis.

INTRODUCTION

So how are you doing, spiritually?

It's such an important question, but it's kind of ambiguous, isn't it? The problem seems to be that everyone has their own definition of "spirituality." To answer the question accurately from God's point of view, we would first have to agree on what he most values and wants from us, then evaluate how we're doing in light of that. So here's how Jesus summarized God's highest priority:

> 29 The most important [commandment of all] is this: ... 30 Love the Lord your God with all your heart and with all your soul and with all your mind and with all your strength. (Mark 12:29-30)

It's simple. What God wants most from us is to love him a certain way. Notice that Jesus didn't merely tell us what to do, he also stressed how to do it—"with all your heart, soul, mind and strength"—as opposed to being only partially interested or occasionally involved.

Seeking to do that consistently well is the nature and emphasis of Christian spirituality.

Often in Scripture, God describes the ideal for our relationship with him by using possessive pronouns like "mine" and "yours."

> "I will walk among you; I will be your God, and you will be my people." (Leviticus 26:12)

> "I will be a Father to you, and you will be my sons and daughters," says the Lord Almighty. (2 Corinthians 6:18)

The kind of love God desires is similar to what we want from our nearest and dearest: loyal, attentive, available, engaged, devoted, affectionate, unconditional and generous. It's not that he wants us to love him only, but to love him fully, first and most. In other words:

God doesn't merely want us to behave or be good; he wants us to be HIS.

That is HUGE! Everything that matters in this life and the next grows out of it becoming so.

Q1: What do you think of that idea, and how does it make you feel?

Q2: How can you tell what a person loves first and most?

POSSIBLE ANSWERS:
- *It's what they usually think and talk about. It preoccupies their attention.*
- *It's what they most want, desire and look forward to.*
- *It's what they work hardest for, pursue, fight for and seek to protect.*
- *It's what they cherish, enjoy and delight in. It gives them the most pleasure.*
- *It's what they spend the most money and time on.*
- *It's what they're least willing to give up, negotiate or compromise on.*
- *It's what they're most concerned, anxious or upset about (possibly) losing.*

Q3: Based on those ideas, what would you say you love most, and how can you tell?

Q4: On average, how much would you say that you love God?

It helps to keep in mind that God never *needs* anything from you or anyone else. He is eternally whole and completely self-sustaining. Even so, he sent his Son here all the way from heaven to convey his love *for* us AND to clarify what he wants most *from* us: to love him back. Doing that well is more important to him than anything else we will ever do.

So what does it mean, and how should we go about it? The Bible reveals at least six distinct ways that we can grow in our experience of God's love for us and how to express ours in response.

SIX GOOD WAYS TO LOVE GOD

1. **Know** Him – Identify him correctly, grow to better understand what he is like and become more personally familiar with him through regular interactions.

2. **Trust** Him – Depend on him for the forgiveness and Life he offers us through Jesus, then remain resolutely confident in him through every difficulty and challenge.

3. **Obey** Him – Endeavor to understand his will and seek to please him at all times, both in heart and in conduct.

4. **Delight in** Him – Cultivate a more constant sense of joyful admiration, pleasure and appreciation for all that he is and does.

5. **Serve** Him – Use your resources to participate with him in the world-repairing, kingdom-building work he is devoted to until Jesus returns.

6. **Love People** – Be conscientiously attentive, compassionate and generous in treating others as Jesus did.

These six activities are a good synopsis-overview of how God wants us to live and express our love for him. They identify six spiritual priorities that everyone who wants to follow Jesus needs to adopt. They are what this book is about, and an entire section with several chapters is devoted to expanding on each one. At any given time, each of us will probably need to pay more attention to one or two of them than the others. But how we're doing at them *all* is a good way to gauge how we're doing spiritually.

Q5: Does it seem to you that anything is missing from the list or doesn't belong on it?

Q6: Which one of the six do you probably need to work on most, and why do you think so?

DO: Memorize the list and try to share it verbatim with someone this week. If you have to cheat or make a mistake, try again *with someone else* until you get it perfect. ❏ Check here once you do.

SECTION ONE

Loving God by KNOWING Him

Ultimately, devising a god of **Y**our **O**wn **U**nderstanding will only produce a version of **YOU**. And that will inevitably pit you against the Bible's description of God.

CHAPTER 1
THREE LEVELS OF ENGAGEMENT

One of the best ways to express our love for God is by desiring and determining to know him. Some think of that as an impossible quest; God is too vast and unlike us to comprehend. So it's common in Western cultures to hear people say things like: "I believe there's *something* (or *someone*) out there, but I'm not sure what. I think of it as a kind of Creative Force or Great Spirit or Higher Power."

We have hundreds of options spread out before us like a giant spiritual buffet. We're told that we no longer have to settle for the religion we were fed when we were young. We're free now to choose whatever appeals to us. "After all," they say:

- "No one person's beliefs are better or worse than anyone else's."

- "They're all equally valid and true, so we should all just agree to **Coexist**."

- "Just come up with something that works for you and go with that: a god of 'Your Own Understanding.'"

> **Q1:** Can you think of reasons why those ideas and that approach might create a problem?

Ultimately, devising a god of **Your Own** Understanding will only produce a version of **YOU**. And that will inevitably pit you against the Bible's description of God.

Notice his response to Moses' question right after Moses learns that he's been volunteered to lead hundreds of thousands of Israelite slaves out of Egypt, right under the Pharaoh's nose.

[13] Moses said to God, "Suppose I go to the Israelites and say to them, 'The God of your fathers has sent me to you,' and they ask me, 'What is his name?' Then what shall I tell them?" [14] God said to Moses, "I AM WHO I AM. This is what you are to say to the Israelites: 'I AM has sent me to you.'" (Exodus 3:13-14)

He's not someone we invent like an imaginary friend. He's the eternal Creator who exists independently of us whether we acknowledge him or not. And he yearns for us to know him in three, increasingly-intimate ways.

Level 1: Recognizing Who He Is and Isn't

Positive Identification

The English still observe an old tradition after their monarch dies and they're preparing to crown a new one. At some point before the actual coronation ceremony, the heir is walked around a group of qualified people who scrutinize his face to make sure it's really him. After all, it would be a bummer if some guy with a wig and makeup managed to make it all the way onto the throne before anyone realizes it's just crazy Uncle Roscoe playing a prank.

How much worse will it be (and has it been) for millions of people to one day discover that the god they have worshiped and trusted to save them isn't really him at all, but some lame impostor or figment of someone's imagination?

To be fair, many insist that will never happen because all the world's religions believe essentially the same thing. They sometimes cite the parable of the six blind people who each examined one part of an elephant and reached drastically different conclusions about what it was like. But the only reason their opinions were contradictory was because none of them had all the information; each had only a portion of the truth. All of them were right in their own way.

Is that the way it is with people's opinions about God? Maybe everyone is right? Do Sikhs, Buddhists, Hindus, Muslims, Confucianists, Jews, Scientologists, Mormons, Christians and so on all believe essentially the same things about God?

Only superficially. I once spoke with a Muslim Uber driver who was raised in Jerusalem and grew up with both Jewish and Christian friends. He said they all got along great as long as they kept their conversations about religion to only an inch deep. Beyond that the differences became glaring. They cannot *all* be right.

So it's critical for us to scrutinize the many interpretations and depictions of God presented to us and be certain that the one we choose is the real deal. We can't build a relationship with the one, true God until we can accurately identify him among all the available options. The first step of knowing him is being able to pick him out of a large line-up of lookalikes and wannabes. The next step is to dig more deeply and, as much as possible, grow in our...

Level 2: Understanding What He's Like

23 This is what the LORD says: "Let not the wise man boast of his wisdom or the strong man boast of his strength or the rich man boast of his riches, 24 but let him who boasts boast about this: that he understands and knows me...."
(Jeremiah 9:23–24a; NIV, '84)

God is impressed with people who care enough to study and learn more about him, what he's like and what's important to him. (More on this shortly.) That can then lead us to the third and most intimate level of knowing, where we actually...

Level 3: Becoming Personally Familiar with Him

Deepening Intimacy

> **Q2:** What kind of things do only good friends and spouses experience and learn about each other as they spend lots of time together?

POSSIBLE ANSWERS:
- *Vulnerability and openness; how they each think and truly feel about all manner of things*
- *What they like and don't like, and why*
- *A deeper interest and concern about what the other is going through*
- *What they can expect and count on from each other*
- *How much they enjoy each other's company*
- *A deep desire to bless, honor, protect and serve each other*

In these and other ways, people who spend lots of quality time together can eventually be said to truly *know* each other. They've become *familiar* with each other and are *close*, perhaps even *intimate*. That's what God wants us to experience in our relationship with him.

> This is eternal life: to know ... the only true God and Jesus Christ, the one (he) sent to earth.
> (John 17:3)

God is too vast and unlike us to comprehend, so we can't know him unless he takes the initiative to reveal himself.

CHAPTER 2
THROUGH FIVE REVEALING SOURCES

God wants everybody to know him by **1.** Recognizing Who He Is and Isn't, **2.** Understanding What He's Like, and **3.** Becoming Personally Familiar with Him. But how on earth *can* we when we can neither see nor hear him?

The answer is that we *can't* unless he takes the initiative to reveal himself to us. So that's what he did, putting himself on display in five, increasingly-specific and personal ways.

Source 1: God Reveals Himself through Created Things

The first way we can know about God is by observing his handiwork. That includes everything in the entire universe, including us humans, from the microscopic to the inter-galactic, both visible and invisible.

[1] The heavens proclaim the glory of God. The skies display his craftsmanship. [2] Day after day they continue to speak; night after night they make him known. [3] They speak without a sound or word; their voice is never heard. [4] Yet their message has gone throughout the earth, and their words to all the world. (Psalm 19:1–4, NLT)

[19] People everywhere can know the truth about God, because he has made it obvious to them. [20] For since the creation of the world, people have been able to understand his eternal power and divine nature by observing what he created. So they have no excuse for not knowing God. (Romans 1:19–20, NLT)

It should be obvious that everything could not have gotten here—or become as it is—all on its own. **A vast, all-powerful super-intelligence must be behind it all.**

*Recognizing God through nature is referred to as **General Revelation** by theologians. Knowing God through Israel's prophets, Jesus, and the message conveyed by his apostles belong in the category of **Special Revelation.***

But if creation is all we have to tell us about God, many things about him remain confusing and unclear. Like:

- How much does he care about us?

- Is life meant to be ruled by "survival of the fittest?"

- What can and can't we count on him to do?

- Is he moody? What makes him happy?

- Does he get angry? Is he angry with me? If so, what makes him so?

- Is he forgiving? If so, how can we please, appease or satisfy him?

- What does he want from us?

Thankfully God didn't limit his self-revelation to what can be known through the generalities of creation. He continued to do so in three additional ways over the course of many centuries, almost always through intermediaries and messengers rather than directly or in person.

Source 2: God Revealed Himself through Israel's Prophets

In the past God spoke to our ancestors through the (Jewish) prophets at many times and in various ways.... (Hebrews 1:1)

*The definition of a **prophet** is "someone who conveys the message of God," whether verbally, in writing or by other creative means.*

- Prophets were not volunteers, but called and appointed by God.

- Prophets spoke and wrote about both the present and the future.

- Prophets were selected from among the descendants of Israel, the "chosen people."[2]

For many centuries when God wanted to communicate or guide his people, he almost always chose someone from among the Jews and employed him as a prophet. The verse in Hebrews you just read tells us a few things about...

How God Revealed Himself to Them:

At Many Times

He didn't do it all at once, but in many pieces and portions, gradually and progressively. His first series of major revelations began through Moses (around 1,400 BC). Those were followed for 1,000 years by a succession of others until Malachi (around 400 BC), followed by 400 years of

---

[2] They weren't "chosen" in the sense of receiving all of God's blessings while the rest of humanity went without. They were chosen to be the first to receive God's detailed self-revelation so they could share him with the rest of the world.

silence until John the Baptist, just prior to Jesus. All their teachings and records were written and preserved for the world in the Jewish Bible that Christians refer to as the Old Testament. *(From here on, "Old Testament" will be abbreviated as "OT" and "New Testament" as "NT.")*

In Various Ways

These included private encounters, audible voices, visions, dreams and their interpretations, angels, supernatural signs, miracles and more.

Via "Inspiration"

Many think the Bible must be full of errors because it was written by fallible men. But before we assume that, another influential factor should be taken into account.

> [16] All Scripture is *inspired ("breathed-out")* by God and is useful for teaching, rebuking, correcting and training in righteousness, [17] so that the servant of God may be thoroughly equipped for every good work. (2 Timothy 3:16–17)

Think of it like this:

> [20] Above all, you must understand that no prophecy of Scripture came about by the prophet's own interpretation of things. [21] For prophecy never had its origin in the human will, but prophets, though human, spoke from God as they were *carried along by the Holy Spirit.* (2 Peter 1:20–21)

Like a sailboat being driven by a strong wind.

How could average bystanders *know* that a so-called prophet was for real? God often validated their credibility by enabling them to perform miracles, and he always made sure that their predictions came true. In fact, if they didn't or if they promoted a different god, he insisted that they be put to death in order to protect Israel from being led astray![3] The people's ability to trust them was that vital.

With those reassurances and safeguards in place, **the Jews cherished, protected and meticulously copied the words of their prophets as sacred, as the words of God himself: the "Holy Bible."** Even more importantly, Jesus arrived later and gave their writings the highest commendation possible.

> [17] "Do not think that I have come to abolish the Law of Moses or the writings of the Prophets *[the OT]*; I have not come to abolish them but to fulfill them. [18] For truly I tell you, until heaven and earth disappear, not the smallest letter, not the least stroke of a pen, will by any means disappear from the Law until everything is accomplished." (Matthew 5:17–18)

---

[3] Deuteronomy 13:1–5; 18:20–22

Israel's prophets made it possible for us to know God in the first, most basic way: by accurately identifying him for us among all of the other available "god-options." As Moses said:

> "The LORD is our God, the LORD alone." (Deuteronomy 6:4b, NLT)

That's a translation of four Hebrew words that say: ***"Yahweh our-God, Yahweh one."*** It highlights two eternal facts about God's identity.

Who God Revealed Himself to Be:

The LORD (Yahweh) Is God

The word "LORD" is all capitalized when it translates the name of God that he revealed to Moses: "Yahweh,"[4] meaning "I am." He always has been and always will be; the Eternal One. By the time of Jesus many regarded that name to be too holy to read or speak aloud, so another word was substituted that meant "Lord." Most modern Bible translators continue to honor that convention and write it as "LORD" so we will recognize it as a reference to Yahweh. It is the primary name God chose to distinguish himself among all the other gods that humans believe in.

> God said to Moses, "Say to the Israelites, 'The LORD (Yahweh), the God of your fathers—the God of Abraham, the God of Isaac and the God of Jacob—has sent me to you.' This is my name forever, the name you shall call me from generation to generation." (Exodus 3:15)

> Do you not know? Have you not heard? The LORD (Yahweh) is the everlasting God, the Creator of the ends of the earth.... (Isaiah 40:28)

He is the exact same one identified in the NT as the God and Father of our Lord Jesus Christ.

Only the LORD (Yahweh) Is God

He's not one of the hundreds of gods invented and worshipped by other peoples. He is one God in particular, and that reality never changes.

> [10] "You are my witnesses," declares the LORD (Yahweh), "and my servant whom I have chosen, so that you may know and believe me and understand that I am he. Before me no god was formed, nor will there be one after me. [11] I, even I, am the LORD, and apart from me there is no savior. [12] I have revealed and saved and proclaimed—I, and not some foreign god among you. You are my witnesses," declares the LORD, "that I am God. [13] Yes, and from ancient days I am he...." (Isaiah 43:10–13)

> "Turn to me and be saved, all you ends of the earth; for I am God, and there is no other." (Isaiah 45:22)

---

[4] A slightly altered Germanic variation of that Hebrew word is "Jehovah."

As arrogant or narrow-minded as it sounds to say it, that means all other belief systems with *different* gods should be rejected as misunderstandings and counterfeits. Their adherents may be genuinely sincere and moral, but that doesn't make them right. Their religions may be ancient and revered by masses, but that doesn't make them true. They have misidentified God and cannot know him until they stand corrected. They are therefore stuck with seeking eternal life and purpose from other sources that are incapable of providing them, so they are spiritually stranded.[5]

Q3: How do these ideas "sit" with you?

The first way God wants us to know him is by recognizing and acknowledging who he is. The second is by growing in our understanding of what he's *like*.

What God Revealed Himself to Be Like:

Israel's prophets repeatedly spotlighted three of God's standout features: He Is **Fearsome**, He Is **Good** and He Is **Great**. The purpose of this book only permits us to dip our toes into these bottomless realities, so consider this an introduction.

God Is FEARSOME

Moses recorded the following events after he led the Jewish people out of slavery in Egypt to meet God "in person" at Mount Sinai.

> [10] The LORD said to Moses, "Go to the people and consecrate them today and tomorrow. Have them wash their clothes [11] and be ready by the third day, because on that day the LORD will come down on Mount Sinai in the sight of all the people. [12] Put limits for the people around the mountain and tell them, 'Be careful that you do not approach the mountain or touch the foot of it. Whoever touches the mountain is to be put to death. [13] They are to be stoned or shot with arrows; not a hand is to be laid on them. No person or animal shall be permitted to live.' Only when the ram's horn sounds a long blast may they approach the mountain."
> [14] After Moses had gone down the mountain to the people, he consecrated them, and they washed their clothes. [15] Then he said to the people, "Prepare yourselves for the third day. Abstain from sexual relations."

---

[5] Of course the statements in this paragraph are only valid if the OT legitimately and accurately contains God's revelation of truth. We haven't yet established that point, but it is based on the belief that Jesus's authority as God's Son was confirmed by his resurrection (Romans 1:4). It therefore follows that his assessment of the OT—as the eternal and unchanging Word of God—is compelling.

¹⁶ On the morning of the third day there was thunder and lightning, with a thick cloud over the mountain, and a very loud trumpet blast. Everyone in the camp trembled. ¹⁷ Then Moses led the people out of the camp to meet with God, and they stood at the foot of the mountain. ¹⁸ Mount Sinai was covered with smoke, because the LORD descended on it in fire. The smoke billowed up from it like smoke from a furnace, and the whole mountain trembled violently. ¹⁹ As the sound of the trumpet grew louder and louder, Moses spoke and the voice of God answered him.
²⁰ The LORD descended to the top of Mount Sinai and called Moses to the top of the mountain. So Moses went up ²¹ and the LORD said to him, "Go down and warn the people so they do not force their way through to see the LORD and many of them perish. ²² Even the priests, who approach the LORD, must consecrate themselves, or the LORD will break out against them."
(Exodus 19:10–22)

Q4: If God wanted to create a close relationship with those people, why do you think he revealed himself as so terrifying, dangerous and unapproachable?

TWO POSSIBLE ANSWERS:

- *Some of it was to contrast himself with the inferior, false gods they had known in Egypt so they wouldn't be tempted to cling or revert to those. He was revealing himself as far more real and awesome than any possible challenger or alternative could ever be. He is "holy"— superior to and "other than" everything else that exists or can be conceived of.*

- ***God's reaction to every kind of impurity and evil is like fire's reaction to gasoline fumes.*** *In order not to incinerate all those people, he needed to persuade them to take him and his commandments seriously. They needed to be strongly dissuaded from disregarding, disrespecting or doing anything that would displease him or provoke his anger. Fear is a strong motivator.*

Bear in mind that the Jews' Mount Sinai encounter with God occurred some 1,400 years before Jesus when God was just *beginning* to reveal himself to people again. The ones he chose to start with were steeped in foreign superstitions. They were also newly independent after centuries of oppression, eager to party and knew almost nothing about him. Recognizing him as gigantic and fearsome was an important starting point for them.

It is for us, as well. Many parts of the Bible speak of fearing God as both appropriate and necessary because of how powerfully it motivates and advises us.

The fear of the LORD is the beginning of wisdom... (Proverbs 9:10)

Through the fear of the LORD evil is avoided. (Proverbs 16:6b)

The fear of the LORD is a fountain of life, turning a person from the snares of death. (Proverbs 14:27)

... What does the LORD your God ask of you but to fear the LORD your God, to walk in obedience to him, to love him, to serve the LORD your God with all your heart and with all your soul. (Deuteronomy 10:12)

So then, are we always supposed to "be afraid" of God? It *depends*.

- The answer is YES if you're strongly inclined to disregard, disobey or wander away from him. His judgments and discipline can be severe.

- But the answer is NO if you're sincerely seeking to love and please him. It's the willfully, persistently defiant child who needs to be afraid of their parent, not the one who is generally submissive and trying to be good but occasionally misbehaves.

Q5: How would you describe your own fear of God?

God's intention is that our fear of him will mature over time into respectful reverence as our relationship becomes more personal and mutually loving. There's a lot more to God than being fearsome. For example...

God Is GOOD

15 Moses said to God, "If your Presence does not go with us, do not send us up from here. 16 How will anyone know that you are pleased with me and with your people unless you go with us? What else will distinguish me and your people from all the other people on the face of the earth?" 17 And the LORD said to Moses, "I will do the very thing you have asked, because I am pleased with you and I know you by name." 18 Then Moses said, "Now show me your **glory**." (Exodus 33:15–18)

Moses wanted to see God in all his unfiltered magnificence and splendor, to have him fully display all that he is without holding anything back.

19 And the LORD said, "I will cause all my **goodness** to pass in front of you, and I will proclaim my name, the LORD, in your presence. I will have mercy on whom I will have mercy, and I will have compassion on whom I will have compassion. 20 But, you cannot see my face, for no one may see me and live." (Exodus 33:19–20)

God declined Moses's request because it would vaporize him like a picnicker on a nuclear bomb test site. So he proposed an alternative.

> 21 Then the LORD said, "There is a place near me where you may stand on a rock. 22 When my glory passes by, I will put you in a cleft in the rock and cover you with my hand until I have passed by. 23 Then I will remove my hand and you will see my back; but my face must not be seen." (Exodus 33:21–23)

At least partly, God's "glory" is the outward appearance of his inner goodness, like intense heat and light are outward expressions of the nuclear fusion occurring in our sun. his goodness is so pure and absolute that it shines out of him as a glorious, exposing and consuming brilliance.

God offered to reveal himself to his prophet in a way that he could survive and pass on to us. He would give him a passing glimpse of his dazzling goodness and then audibly describe what Moses couldn't bear to see.

> 4 So Moses chiseled out two stone tablets like the first ones and went up Mount Sinai early in the morning, as the LORD had commanded him; and he carried the two stone tablets in his hands. 5 Then the LORD came down in the cloud and stood there with him and proclaimed his name, the LORD. 6 And he passed in front of Moses, proclaiming, "The LORD, the LORD, the compassionate and gracious God, slow to anger, abounding in love and faithfulness, 7 maintaining love to thousands, and forgiving wickedness, rebellion and sin. Yet he does not leave the guilty unpunished; he punishes the children and their children for the sin of the parents to the third and fourth generation." 8 Moses bowed to the ground at once and worshiped. (Exodus 34:4–8)

That's a description of how the glorious light of God's goodness refracts into a rainbow of radiant qualities. They reveal him to be two things in particular: *1. Loving* and *2. Just*.

He Is Loving

In Exodus 34:6–7a, God first says his goodness consists of the kind of love that shows up in numerous, beautiful ways as he deals with his children.

- **He Is Compassionate** — He feels tender concern when he see someone in need, like what a mother feels for her nursing infant, and it stirs him to provide for them.

- **He Is Gracious** — He delights to give and bless, to show kindness and to extend mercy to the undeserving.

- **He Is Slow to Anger** — He's not easily annoyed or short-tempered, but tolerant and patient. He remembers that we are only dust and need lots of do-overs to get things right.

- **He Abounds in Love and Faithfulness** — God is reliably loyal in his commitment to care for us and keep his promises. He will never leave or forsake us, no matter how many times we let him down.

- **He Maintains Love to Thousands** — He's not limited to a preferred few, but loves each and every one of us in a "till death do us part" kind of commitment. Heaven will be filled with more people than we can count.

- **He Forgives Wickedness, Rebellion and Sin** — Every kind of wrong we can think of is catalogued under those three terms. How does God respond when those he loves do things he hates? When they repent, he forgives them. Not reluctantly, but eagerly and repeatedly. The death of God's Son made his full and eternal pardon available to the worst of us for the worst we can do.[6]

All six of those descriptions tell us something of what God is like. They are facets of what the prophets meant when they referred to him throughout the OT as "loving." He wants us to know and count on them to be true about him, because we *need* them to be.

Q6: Which of those half-dozen descriptions of God's love do you most appreciate, and why?

A word of caution is in order here. As wonderful and comprehensive as God's love is, we need to be careful not to misrepresent it. Many people stumble at this point by concluding that God is **all** and **only** loving. They say things like, "My God would never judge or punish or send anyone to hell." But the truth they fail to grasp is that God's goodness is *more* than "loving." In addition:

He Is Just

He always does what is right and fair. He never ignores, minimizes or allows sin and wrongdoing to remain unaddressed. In fact, they arouse the fierce part of his goodness that is determined to punish those who *should* be punished, to protect what is beautiful and to defend those he loves. The unrepentant *must* be confronted and dealt with as they deserve.

(Though he abundantly loves and forgives,) yet he does not leave the guilty unpunished; he punishes the children and their children for the sin of the parents to the third and fourth generation. (Exodus 34:7b)

None of us gets to blame anyone else for our moral failures, even if we were shaped, damaged or scarred by wickedness in our past. He will be completely understanding and take everything relevant into account, but each of us will still answer to God for deliberately dishonoring and

---

[6] I highly recommend the book *Knowing God*, by J.I. Packer for his deep and rich exploration of these qualities.

disobeying him. In the end he will quarantine and dispose of all evil in hell, a place created to be the final destiny for the devil and his angels.[7] And everyone in heaven, including us, will praise and thank him for finally doing so.[8]

How then should we think about the widespread belief that God's love will prevent him from judging and punishing people? By remembering that, because he is truly Good, he is *more* than Loving; he is also *Just*. The two of those attributes together make him glorious.

Loving + Just = Good

Q7: What concerns or questions come to your mind as you consider these ideas?

Before we finish this segment on what God is *like*, let's glance at a third, all-encompassing attribute that contributes to his glory.

God Is GREAT

Great is the LORD and most worthy of praise; his greatness no one can fathom. (Psalm 145:3)

From Genesis to Malachi the OT prophets reveal God to be the greatest conceivable being. Recognizing his *greatness* along with his *fearsomeness* and *goodness* is an indispensable part of getting to know him as he is.

He inherently *possesses* all sorts of qualities that make him awesome, many of which are briefly defined below. All of them are mind-expanding and awe-inspiring to contemplate. As you read through the entire list, underline three or four you find to be *especially* important or interesting. Then go back through those in particular, read/reflect on the verses that accompany them and talk to God about what they say. You can look up the others later if you wish; there's gold in them.

- **Eternal** – *no beginning or end; fully present in every moment of time simultaneously* (Psalm 90:2–4; Isaiah 57:15; Jude 25; Revelation 1:8)

- **Self-existing** – *no source, cause or reason for existence outside of himself* (Exodus 3:14; John 5:26)

---

[7] Matthew 25:41, 46; Revelation 20:10
[8] Revelation 11:15-18

- **Omnipresent** – *completely present everywhere at once; without boundaries*
  (Jeremiah 23:23–24; Psalms 139:7–8)

- **Holy** – *other than, above and unlike any other; set apart from all that is impure or defiled; not common; sacred*
  (Isaiah 6:1–3; 1 Timothy 6:16; 1 Peter 1:15–16; Hebrews 12:14)

- **Perfect/Unchangeable** – *incapable of improvement*
  (Psalm 102:25–27; Matthew 5:48)

- **Sovereign** – *has the right to do whatever pleases him and continually exercises it by ruling over all creation*
  (Lamentations 3:37–38; Ephesians 1:11; Colossians 1:16–17)

- **Beautiful** – *fully possesses all desirable qualities*
  (Psalms 27:4; 73:25)

- **Independent** – *never needs anything*
  (Job 41:11; Psalm 50:10–12; Acts 17:24–25)

- **Omniscient** – *always knows and is fully aware of everything at once, both actual and possible*
  (Isaiah 46:9–10; Hebrews 4:13; Matthew 10:29–30)

- **All-wise** – *always knows and chooses the best means and ends*
  (Romans 8:28–29; 16:27; James 1:5)

- **Omnipotent** – *all-powerful; able to do and accomplish whatever he wills*
  (Psalm 115:3; Jeremiah 32:27; Ephesians 3:20)

Q8: Which two of the qualities on that list interest or amaze you most, and why?

The best way for us to know and understand God is by familiarizing ourselves with Jesus.

CHAPTER 3
SOURCE 3: God Revealed Himself through JESUS

It may seem that God is hidden, but the problem is usually with our faulty spiritual sensors, not with him. *You can't find buried diamonds using a metal detector, even if they're right under your nose.* He has left unmistakable evidence of his divine genius and power everywhere we look in his creation. He has also revealed himself even *more* explicitly through the timeless words of Israel's prophets that are preserved in the OT portion of our Bibles.

But there are hard limits on how well you can know someone by reading or hearing about them. I met the woman who became my wife online through a dating website that only allowed us to write each other over the first few weeks. I could tell from the 2" x 2" picture I received via email that she was pretty and her dog was cute. But it didn't take long to realize we needed more than that to develop a real connection.

Likewise with God. That's why, at just the right moment in human history, he took a giant step closer to us by revealing himself in another way that few imagined he would: as one of us!

Along with displaying God's love, Jesus addressed people as though he possessed supreme authority. He expected them to believe that the eternal Creator was constantly acting and speaking through him. He regularly introduced his statements with the word(s), "Amen, amen." In other words, "You can be absolutely confident that what I'm about to tell you is the God's-honest truth."

> 7 [Jesus said,] "If you really know me, you will know my Father as well.... 24b These words you hear are not my own; they belong to the Father who sent me." (John 14:7, 24b)

The Bible portrays him as occupying an entirely different level than all the other prophets who came before and after him, as the NT writer of Hebrews plainly stated.

Jesus's Revelation Was Final

> 1 In the past God spoke to our ancestors through the prophets at many times and in various ways, 2a but in these last days he has spoken to us by his Son.... (Hebrews 1:1–2a)

The words, "God *has spoken* by his Son" denote the *finality* of what he had to say. The progression of God's self-disclosure in human history reached its climax and fulfillment in him. Jesus put it like this in a mind-blowing interaction with one of his disciples:

> [8] Philip said (to Jesus), "Lord, show us the Father and that will be enough for us." [9] Jesus answered: "Don't you know me, Philip, even after I have been among you such a long time? Anyone who has seen me has seen the Father. How can you say, 'Show us the Father'? [10] Don't you believe that I am in the Father, and that the Father is in me? The words I say to you I do not speak on my own authority. Rather, it is the Father, living in me, who is doing his work." (John 14:8–10)

> No one has ever seen God, but the one and only Son, who is himself God and is in closest relationship with the Father, has made him known. (John 1:18)

What makes Jesus superior to the many other spiritual teachers and leaders who ever lived? Why is *his* revelation of God better—more authoritative and right—than everyone else's? The answer is presented in the Bible's explanation of who Jesus actually was.

Jesus's Credentials Were Exceptional

He possessed certain qualifications that no other human being could ever acquire. Here are four:

He Was the "Son of Man"

Being "*a* son of man" simply refers to being human/mortal, flesh and blood, a son of Adam. The NT strongly affirms the idea that Jesus was as fully human as you or I (Hebrews 2:17–18).

But that's not the phrase Jesus used. He *never* referred to himself as *"a"* son of man. Instead he referred to himself as *"the"* son of man. Over eighty recorded times! That was his favorite self-designation. He understood himself to be unique among the rest of us.

> "I want you to know that the Son of Man has authority on earth to forgive sins." (Matthew 9:6)

> [27] ... "The Sabbath was made (by God) for man, not man for the Sabbath. [28] So the Son of Man is Lord even of the Sabbath." (Mark 2:27–28)

> [26] As the Father has life in himself, so he has granted the Son also to have life in himself. [27] And he has given him authority to judge because he is the Son of Man. (John 5:26–27; see Matthew 25:31-46 for more on this)

Add to those verses the exalted imagery in Daniel 7:13–14 of "one like a Son of Man" who is welcomed into the presence of "the Ancient of Days," is "given authority, glory and sovereign power" over an indestructible kingdom, and who is worshiped by "all nations and peoples of every language." Jesus owned *all* of that as referring to him!

So he was not merely one of us. **He was Chief among us.** He was and is the Leader, Head, Representative and Judge of the entire human race. Jesus was not just "a" man, but **"the"** man. And *more*.

He Was the "Son of David" / Messiah

David was king over Israel around 1000 B.C. He led the nation into its Golden Age and exalted Yahweh as their God in a true theocracy.

Through the prophet Nathan, God promised David that one of his descendants would also become king, pick up where he left off, expand the borders of his reign to reach the ends of the earth, and preside over *another* Golden Age more glorious than the first.

> "Your house and your kingdom will endure forever before me; your throne will be established forever." (2 Samuel 7:16)

Four hundred years afterwards (around 600 B.C.), the prophet Jeremiah reiterated that promise:

> 5 "The days are coming," declares the LORD (Yahweh), "when I will raise up for David a righteous Branch, a King who will reign wisely and do what is just and right in the land…. 6b This is the name by which he will be called: The LORD (Yahweh) Our Righteous Savior." (Jeremiah 23:5–6b; Psalm 89:36 adds, "his dynasty will go on forever; his kingdom will endure as the sun.")

That future-world King to be chosen and exalted by God was referred to elsewhere as the *"Anointed One."* That's a translation of both the Hebrew word "Messiah" and the Greek word "Christ." It often referred to a King. Centuries later …

> 26b … God sent the angel Gabriel to Nazareth, a town in Galilee, 27 to a virgin pledged to be married to a man named Joseph, a descendant of David…. 30 The angel said to her, "Do not be afraid, Mary; you have found favor with God. 31 You will conceive and give birth to a son, and you are to call him Jesus. 32 He will be great and will be called the Son of the Most High. The Lord God will give him the throne of his father David, 33 and he will reign over Jacob's (Israel's) descendants forever; his kingdom will never end." (Luke 1:26b–33)

After Jesus grew up and went public, he believed it was critically important for his closest followers to recognize this about him, so he asked them:

> 13b … "Who do people say the Son of Man is?" 14 They replied, "Some say John the Baptist; others say Elijah; and still others, Jeremiah or one of the prophets." 15 "But what about you?" he asked. "Who do you say I am?" 16 Simon Peter answered, "You are the Messiah (Christ), the Son of the living God." 17 Jesus replied, "Blessed are you, Simon son of Jonah, for this was not revealed to you by flesh and blood, but by my Father in heaven." (Matthew 16:13b–17)

So "Christ" wasn't Jesus's last name, it was his *title*: "God's anointed one," Messiah/Christ Jesus. He, the Son of Man, was also the son of David, the One appointed by God to rule earth as its glorious King. The crown fit perfectly, and he was pleased to wear it.

A third credential Jesus possessed also identified him as superior in rank and worthy of greater honor than the rest of us:

He Was the "Son of God"

16 For we did not follow cleverly devised stories when we told you about the coming of our Lord Jesus Christ in power, but we were eyewitnesses of his majesty. 17 He received honor and glory from God the Father when the voice came to him from the Majestic Glory, saying, "This is my Son, whom I love; with him I am well pleased." 18 We ourselves heard this voice that came from heaven when we were with him on the sacred mountain. (2 Peter 1:16–18)

That experience probably settled any remaining doubt those disciples had about Jesus's identity. So did Jesus's own statements while being interrogated before his execution:

61 (At the end of Jesus's trial,) the high priest asked him, "Are you the Messiah/Christ, the Son of the Blessed One?" 62 "I am," said Jesus. "And you will see the Son of Man sitting at the right hand of the Mighty One and coming on the clouds of heaven." (Mark 14:61b–62)

The Son of Man who was the son of David (the Messiah/Christ) was also the Son of God! Which made and makes him uniquely able to reveal God so we can know him. But nothing qualifies Jesus more than his ultimate credential.

He Was "God the Son"

In the eighth chapter of John's gospel, Jesus had a disturbing dialog with a skeptical audience. In it he made an astonishing statement about Abraham, the father of the Jewish people/faith who lived 2,000 years before Jesus's birth.

56 "Your father Abraham rejoiced at the thought of seeing my day; he saw it and was glad."
57 "You are not yet fifty years old," they said to him, "and you have seen Abraham!" 58 "Very truly I tell you," Jesus answered, "before Abraham was born, I am!" 59 At this, they picked up stones to stone him, but Jesus hid himself, slipping away from the temple grounds. (John 8:56–59)

Jesus had a way of making his listeners so sputtering mad they wanted to crush him. His final statement in that speech made them boil over because of what they understood him to mean by it. They were familiar with the account of the burning bush in Exodus 3 when God identified himself to Moses by using the name "I am." And here's how they explained their violent reaction against Jesus:

"We are not stoning you for any good work, but for blasphemy, because you, a mere man, claim to be God." (John 10:33)

Indeed, he did. Many times and in various ways. It still sounds wrong to most people. But those who knew and trusted him cherished it as the insight that would change their world and set them free. Here was their point: **God didn't merely reveal himself to us *THROUGH* Jesus, but *AS* Jesus. In him the invisible God became incarnate and visible.** Remember how Jesus summarized it to Phillip:

"Anyone who has seen me has seen the Father. So why are you asking me to show him to you?" (John 14:9b, NLT)

But how could that be literally true? How could someone be the infinite, eternal, all-powerful Creator and a true, finite human being at the same time? How could God be here on earth as the man, Jesus, and simultaneously be in heaven as God? How could Jesus pray to God as his Father and yet also be God, himself?

In a humbly satisfying way, the answer is impossible for us to comprehend! It binds together two realities that cannot coherently co-exist in our ant-size brains. We must rely on the settled conclusions of Jesus's trusted apprentices, several of which are included in the Supplements on the two next pages.

A FAMOUS CHALLENGE

In his famous book, Mere Christianity, C.S. Lewis added: "One of the really foolish things that people often say about Jesus is: 'I'm ready to accept him as a great moral teacher, but I don't accept his claim to be God.' That is the one thing we must not say. A man who was merely a man and said the sort of things Jesus said would not be a great moral teacher. He would either be a lunatic—on the level with the man who says he is a poached egg—or else he would be the Devil of Hell. You must make your choice. Either this man was, and is, the Son of God; or else a madman or something worse. You can shut him up for a fool, you can spit at him and kill him as a demon, or you can fall at his feet and call him Lord and God. But let us not come up with any patronizing nonsense about his being a great human teacher. He has not left that open to us. He did not intend to."[9]

In Jesus's own words: "I am the Alpha and the Omega, the First and the Last, the Beginning and the End." (Revelation 22:13)

---

[9] C.S. Lewis, *Mere Christianity* (Harper San Francisco, 1952), p. 56

SUPPLEMENT A - AFFIRMATIONS OF JESUS'S IDENTITY AS *"GOD THE SON"*

1. [1] [On the night before his crucifixion, with his disciples present,] Jesus looked toward heaven and prayed: "Father, the hour has come. Glorify your Son, that your Son may glorify you. [2] For you granted him authority over all people that he might give eternal life to all those you have given him. [3] Now this is eternal life: that they know you, the only true God, and Jesus Christ, whom you have sent. [4] I have brought you glory on earth by finishing the work you gave me to do. [5] And now, Father, glorify me in your presence with the glory I had with you before the world began." (John 17:1–5)

KEY POINT: Jesus believed that he existed before he came to earth, that he shared the glory of God during that time, and that eternal life is something we can only obtain from the Father and the Son, *together*. His disciples also came to believe this:

[1] That which was from the beginning, which we have heard, which we have seen with our eyes, which we have looked at and our hands have touched—this we proclaim concerning the Word of life. [2] The life appeared; we have seen it and testify to it, and we proclaim to you the eternal life, which was with the Father and has appeared to us. (1 John 1:1–2)

2. [2] ... In these last days (God) has spoken to us by his Son, whom he appointed heir of all things, and through whom also he made the universe. [3] The Son is the radiance of God's glory and the exact representation of his being, sustaining all things by his powerful word. ... [6] When God brings his first-born into the world, he says, "Let all God's angels worship him." [7] In speaking of the angels he says, "He makes his angels spirits, and his servants flames of fire." [8] But about the Son he says, "Your throne, O God, will last for ever and ever; a scepter of justice will be the scepter of your kingdom." (Hebrews 1:2–8)

KEY POINTS:

Verse 3a– To say that Jesus is *"the radiance of God's glory"* means he is to God what heat and light are to the sun. (*Compare the account of Jesus's transfiguration in Matthew 17:1–8 and how he is described in Revelation 1:12–18.*)

Verse 3b– *"The exact representation of God's being"* is like the perfect impression of a signet ring in warm wax. In this case, God became ("incarnated" himself in) a human being.

Verse 6– Jesus is as worthy of worship as God himself! The term "firstborn" does not mean "first to be born or created," but rather "preeminent and foremost; first above all others."

Verse 8 – Jesus is addressed as "God" by God himself!

3. No one has ever seen God, but the one and only Son, who is himself God and is in closest relationship with the Father, has made him known. (John 1:18)

4. [15] The Son is the image of the invisible God, the firstborn over all creation. [16] For in him all things were created: things in heaven and on earth, visible and invisible, whether thrones or powers or rulers or authorities; all things have been created through him and for him. [17] He is before all things, and in him all things hold together. (Colossians 1:15–17)

5. [6] (Christ Jesus), being in very nature God, did not consider equality with God something to be used to his own advantage; [7] rather, he made himself nothing by taking the very nature of a servant, being made in human likeness. [8] And being found in appearance as a man, he humbled himself by becoming obedient to death — even death on a cross! [9] Therefore God exalted him to the highest place and gave him the name that is above every name, [10] that at the name of Jesus every knee should bow, in heaven and on earth and under the earth, [11] and every tongue acknowledge that Jesus Christ is Lord, to the glory of God the Father. (Philippians 2:6–11)

SUPPLEMENT B – AN ATTEMPT TO EXPLAIN AND VISUALIZE THE "TRINITY"

GOD IS A UNITY OF ONE

God Is a Single Divine Being

Hear O Israel: The LORD (Yahweh) is our God, the LORD (Yahweh) is one! (Deuteronomy 6:4)

This is what the LORD says — Israel's King and Redeemer, the LORD Almighty: "I am the first and I am the last; apart from me there is no God." (Isaiah 44:6)

There is one God and one mediator between God and mankind, the man Christ Jesus. (1 Timothy 2:5)

GOD IS A PLURALITY OF THREE - A "TRI-UNITY"

Three Distinct "Persons" Are Identified as God (and equally share his divine nature)

- *1. The Father*– Genesis 1:1; Ephesians 4:6; etc.
- *2. The Word or Son*– John 1:1–5, 14; Titus 2:13; 2 Peter 1:1; see "Supplement A" on page 36 for more.
- *3. The Holy Spirit*– Acts 5:3–4; 1 Corinthians 2:10–11; 3:16.
- *All 3 are God*– Matthew 28:19; 2 Corinthians 13:14; Ephesians 4:4–6; 1 Peter 1:2; Jude 20–21.
- The one God's inherent plurality is implied in passages like Genesis 1:26–27; 3:22; 11:7; Isaiah 6:8; Psalm 45:6–7 (quoted in Hebrews 1:8); and Psalm 110:1 (cited by Jesus in Matthew 22:41–46).

ONE PERSON OF THIS "TRINITY" BECAME HUMAN

[1] In the beginning was the Word, and the Word was with God, and the Word was God. [2] He was with God in the beginning. [3] Through him all things were made; without him nothing was made that has been made... (John 1:1–3)

The angel told Mary, "The Holy Spirit will come on you, and the power of the Most High will overshadow you. So the holy one to be born will be called the Son of God." (Luke 1:35)

The Word became flesh and made his dwelling among us. We have seen his glory, the glory of the One and Only Son, who came from the Father, full of grace and truth. (John 1:14)

CONCLUSION: There is no explanation for the Trinity or Jesus's dual nature that makes completely logical sense to us. We are way out of our depth. Our finite minds cannot fathom the nature of a divine being, but what we can understand should be sufficient to inspire our worship.

As noted a few pages back, C. S. Lewis suggested that there are only three conclusions we can reach about Jesus– "Lord, Liar, or Lunatic". Some say a fourth possibility should be added— "Legend." This one argues that the NT portrayals of Jesus as a God-man were invented or altered to make him seem like more than he was. That raises the crucial question of whether or not we can trust *any* of the NT as an accurate record of Jesus's life and teachings. If not, *everything* it says is doubtful.

We will tackle that objection in Chapter 4. For now you can rest assured that every detail of it has been scrutinized and debated by scholars for hundreds of years. *Many* with impeccable qualifications have concluded that the NT is *remarkably* trustworthy, and the Jesus it presents is identical to the actual, historical Jesus.[10]

Q9: What do you think of the reasoning that there are only four options available to us when it comes to Jesus's identity?

Q10: Why was it so important to Jesus (and the biblical writers) for us to be clear about his true identity? What difference does it make if we get that right or not?

If it's true that Jesus rightfully possessed all four of the credentials noted above—the Son of Man, Son of David, Son of God and God the Son—it follows that he and his revelation of God are infinitely and permanently superior to everyone else's. Therefore, the best way for us to understand and know God is by familiarizing ourselves with Jesus.

No one has ever seen God, but the one and only Son, who is himself God and is in closest relationship with the Father, has made him known. (John 1:18)

---

[10] If you're curious or skeptical about that, the following books go into satisfying detail about the processes by which it was written, preserved and assembled.
- *Why I Trust the Bible*, William D. Mounce (Grand Rapids: Zondervan, 2021), 269 pages; excellent and thorough
- *Seven Reasons Why You Can Trust the Bible*, Erwin Lutzer (Chicago: Moody, 2015), 248 pages; a popular, layperson's approach
- *Reinventing Jesus: What the Da Vinci Code & Other Novel Speculations Don't Tell You*, J. Ed Komoszewski, M. James Sawyer and Daniel B. Wallace (Grand Rapids: Kregel, 2006), 347 pages; very in-depth
- *Evidence That Demands a Verdict: Life-Changing Truth for a Skeptical World*, Josh & Sean McDowell (Nashville: Thomas Nelson, 2017), Chapter 3, 41–91; a shorter but solid presentation in a large book that answers many additional questions you may wonder about

31 ... Jesus said, "If you hold to my teaching, you are really my disciples. 32 Then you will know the truth, and the truth will set you free." (John 8:31b)

Q11: Do you have any reservations or questions about anything you just read?

Is it conceivable that God could perfectly coordinate his self-revelation to the human race through Jesus, then utterly fumble its final hand-off to incompetent couriers?

CHAPTER 4
SOURCE 4: God Revealed Himself through JESUS'S APOSTLES

It's all great that God showed up in person to reveal himself to us through Jesus. But we obviously don't have the same kind of access to him that people did back then. Face-to-face lunches by the lake have been cancelled for the time being. So how are *we* supposed to learn from him what he came to communicate?

All along his plan was to carefully select an inner circle of 12 eager students, give them everything he had, and then send them out to share it with the rest of us.

They Possessed Jesus's Spirit and Authority

[On the night before his crucifixion, Jesus told his disciples,] "When the Father sends the Advocate as my representative—that is, the Holy Spirit—he will teach you everything and will remind you of everything I have told you." (John 14:26)

[After his resurrection,] Jesus told his disciples, "You will receive power when the Holy Spirit comes upon you. And you will be my witnesses, telling people about me everywhere—in Jerusalem, throughout Judea, in Samaria, and to the ends of the earth." (Acts 1:8 NLT)

[18] Then Jesus came to them and said, "All authority in heaven and on earth has been given to me. [19] Therefore [you are to] go and make disciples of all nations, baptizing them in the name of the Father and of the Son and of the Holy Spirit, [20] and teaching them to obey everything I have commanded you. And surely I am with you always, to the very end of the age." (Matthew 28:18–20)

Their Words Were God's (= "Inspired")

[3] The appeal we (apostles) make does not spring from error or impure motives, nor are we trying to trick you. [4] On the contrary, we speak as those approved by God to be entrusted with the **gospel**. We are not trying to please people but God, who tests our hearts. [8] ...Because we loved you so much, we were delighted to share with you

*The word **Gospel** means "good news." God's gospel is that his forgiveness and eternal life are now available to us through faith in Jesus.*

not only the gospel of God but our lives as well. ...[13] And we also thank God continually because, when you received the word of God, which you heard from us, you accepted it not as a human word, but as it actually is, the word of God, which is indeed at work in you who believe. (1 Thessalonians 2:3–13)

Everyone was filled with awe at the many wonders and signs performed by the apostles. (Acts 2:43)

Paul and Barnabas spent considerable time there, speaking boldly for the Lord, who confirmed the message of his grace by enabling them to perform signs and wonders. (Acts 14:3)

[19] You (non-Jews) are no longer foreigners and strangers (to God's covenants), but fellow citizens with God's (Jewish) people and also members of his household, [20] built on the foundation of the apostles (NT) and prophets (OT), with Christ Jesus himself as the chief cornerstone. (Ephesians 2:19–20)

If you have doubts about the NT's credibility, quoting it to prove its own divine inspiration will not be very persuasive to you. Part of this issue will be resolved as you learn how its original writings were copied and preserved until now. But why should we believe that its authors were inspired by God and completely accurate in the first place?

The short answer is the same as in footnote 5 referring to the OT. The historically credible event of Jesus's resurrection validates his authority as God's representative. And the historically credible evidence that this risen Jesus commissioned his apostles to publish his message confirms their authority as God's spokesmen. That is why we can fully trust everything they spoke and wrote.

Former skeptic and NT scholar Dr. Jonathan Lunde stated it perfectly: "The historical event (not a mere claim) grounds the authority of Jesus. And the authority of Jesus validates the authority of the Bible. That is why, if someone could convince me that Jesus did not rise from the dead, I would no longer hold to the Bible as absolute truth."

Their Words Were Preserved

This is the topic discussed in footnote 10. Here is a summary of what you'll learn by reading the books recommended there:

1. Christians always needed to discern which of the religious writings available were inspired by God as they met to worship and learn. As persecution intensified in the second and third centuries, they also had to decide which writings to protect at all costs. They chose all of the apostles' books and letters that are still included in our NTs.

2. From the second through the fourth century, most Christian leaders affirmed a 27-book "canon" (official collection) that possessed "apostolic authority."[11] At the Council of Hippo in AD 393, 70 respected elders met and formally endorsed the long-standing

[11] According to the ancient church historian, Eusebius, described in the Wikipedia article, "Development of the New Testament Canon."

belief that those 27 writings—and *only* them—were to be revered along with the books of the OT as inspired by God.[12]

3. All 27 NT books were originally written in Greek on perishable material. No originals survived, but they were copied and recopied for hundreds of years.

4. Over 5,600 ancient copies of those books still exist, either whole or in portions and fragments. They contain a large number of discrepancies ("variants") between them. But...

5. From that huge collection of copies, modern textual critics[13] have reconstructed a standardized Greek NT[14] accepted by most scholars to be about 99% (+/- .5%) identical to the original. None of the remaining uncertainties affect a crucial Christian teaching.

6. Nearly all modern, widely-distributed translations are very accurate versions of the original Greek (although they may use different translation approaches).

7. God's self-revelation through Jesus has been fully and faithfully passed down to us in the 27 writings of his chosen apostles and a few of their close associates.

> **Q12:** Can you think of a reason or two why you need to know the things you read in the last several pages, and when you might need them?

Conclusion

Our Bibles contain the inspired words of God originally given to the prophets of Israel, to Jesus Christ and to Jesus's apostles. We can read them and learn about him with confidence that we are accessing the Original Source.

How then should we regard all other teachers and writings that claim to add something missing or to correct something mistaken in the Bible?

> [24] False messiahs and false prophets will rise up and perform great signs and wonders so as to deceive, if possible, even God's chosen ones. [25] See, I have warned you about this ahead of time. (Matthew 24:24–25 NLT)

---

[12] During the 300 years before that Council, Christians had used at least four criteria to determine if a writing was inspired by God or not:
- It claimed to be divinely authorized, either explicitly or implicitly.
- It was written by an accredited apostle of Christ or one of their close associates who faithfully represented their teachings.
- It was consistently factual and harmonized with other writings already accepted as inspired.
- It was widely recognized and accepted by the people of God as possessing the authority and life-transforming power of God.

[13] Textual critics employ standardized rules and methods to ascertain the original wording of an ancient text by examining its copies.

[14] Nestle-Aland Novum Testamentum Graece, 28th rev. ed. (NA28) (Stuttgart: German Bible Society, 2012).

8 Even if we (apostles) or an angel from heaven should preach a gospel other than the one we preached to you, let them be under God's curse! 9 As we have already said, so now I say again: If anybody is preaching to you a gospel other than what you accepted, let them be under God's curse! (Galatians 1:8–9)

Dear friends, I had been eagerly planning to write to you about the salvation we all share. But now I find that I must write about something else, urging you to defend *("contend strenuously in defense of")* the faith that God has entrusted once for all time to his holy people. (Jude 3 NLT)

Q13: What does that last verse say about "the faith," and what does it suggest to you?

Q14: Can you name at least three current groups or teachers with lots of followers that we should be concerned about because they have altered "the faith?"

Q15: What are some specific beliefs held by those groups and teachers that contradict the Word of God?

Q16: How should we respond to them?

[24] The Lord's servant must not be quarrelsome but must be kind to everyone, able to teach, not resentful *(or reactive)*. [25] Opponents must be gently instructed, in the hope that God will grant them repentance leading them to a knowledge of the truth, [26] and that they will come to their senses and escape from the trap of the devil, who has taken them captive to do his will. (2 Timothy 2:24–26)

Q17: Do you still have unanswered questions about God revealing himself through Jesus's apostles and their writings? If so, write them here:

Following Jesus' example may require you to rise earlier or retire later or hide awhile in your car, but making it a habit will be one of the best things you ever do.

CHAPTER 5
SOURCE 5: God Reveals Himself through DIRECT ENCOUNTERS

For thousands of years God has been showing himself to the human race through creation, prophets, Jesus and Jesus's apostles. It's clear that he wants very much for us to know him:

- First, by recognizing him as the only real God among many inferior pretenders.

- Second, by understanding as much as possible what he's truly like.

- Third, by frequently interacting with him in a personal way that enables us to become more familiar and intimate. That is the prize he's been after all along, both for our sake and his.

… I consider everything a loss compared to the surpassing greatness of knowing Christ Jesus my Lord. (Philippians 3:8a NIV, '84)

Whom have I in heaven but you? And earth has nothing I desire besides you. (Psalm 73:25)

You will fill me with joy in your presence, with eternal pleasures at your right hand. (Psalm 16:11b)

But most of us already have a lot going on with tending to our family, making a living, saving for the future, handling problems and finding time for fun and relaxation. One great enemy of undistracted time alone with God is busyness—what one writer referred to as "the tyranny of the urgent."

Jesus often faced the same adversary. On many days needy people pressed in, wanting a piece of him, and sometimes it got so intense there was no time to eat. But Luke 5:16 says he found a way to counteract that pressure: *"He often withdrew to lonely places and prayed."* Following his example may require you to rise earlier or retire later or hide awhile in a car, but making it a habit will be one of the best things you ever do.

> *This chapter stresses solitude, prayer and Scripture as key ways to engage with God. Many Christians suggest supplementing those with fasting, silence, worship, celebration, community, simplicity, sacrifice and others.*

Encountering God in Prayer

God wants to spend frequent times alone with you that last more than two minutes. He is always focused on you, even when you might prefer privacy. But it can seem strange talking into the air toward someone you can't see or hear. Praying is an exercise of faith that doesn't always affect how you feel. It's how you consciously turn your attention to God and include him in things that matter to you instead of carrying on as though no one is there. If you follow Jesus's example and stay at it, you'll soon discover that it escorts you into a sweet place where the "curtain" concealing heaven grows thinner and God's presence becomes more apparent.

Don't think of praying as a ritual you have to do a certain way, using just the right posture and words. Simply tell God what's on your mind. Talk to him about who and what concerns you. Go into detail. He invites you to unburden your soul. The OT book of Psalms is filled with stirring prayers that you can read aloud in all kinds of situations when you're unsure what to say.

You may experience times when an idea or a person will come to mind with unique force or clarity as you're praying. Don't be quick to dismiss it or move on. On some occasions God will directly "speak" a word of encouragement, guidance or correction to you. On others he will make you aware of someone you should talk with, lend a hand to or pray for. Stay open to the possibility that he may have something specific he wants to convey to you, and pause occasionally to listen for it.

The best advice is to apply Jesus's teaching on how to pray in Matthew 6:5–15. The model prayer that begins in verse nine isn't simply meant to be repeated. Think of it as an outline or a black and white sketch waiting for you to add some color. Each of its parts provides a distinct topic or request for you to ponder and expand-on in your own words. Use them as conversation starters to get you talking with God about things that deserve your focused attention. Things like these:

GOD'S ROLE - *"Our Father in heaven"* (v. 9a)

He is not just *God* to us, any more than we are just *people* to our children. We are "above" them in some ways, but we are primarily their loving parents, their moms and dads, and we want them to know us as such. God desires something comparable. Though he is far above us in heaven, he mostly wants us to know him as a good and attentive father who treasures us as his children.

GOD'S HONOR - *"Hallowed be your name"* (v. 9b)

God actually cares about how people think of him; not because he has a fragile ego, but because how we *regard* him governs how we relate to him. He therefore wants us to *regard* his "name"— which represents all that he *is*—as "hallowed." The word means *holy, set apart, sacred.* When used of God it describes someone who is so distinctive and extraordinary, so pure and beautiful, so awesome and glorious and magnificent, that he deserves to be honored with the utmost respect, even reverence and adoration. Part of our time in prayer is best spent considering, admiring, praising and appreciating the things which make our Father worthy of such lofty adjectives.

GOD'S RULE - *"May your kingdom come"* (v. 10a)

Many people believe God is totally in charge of the world, but that is not the complete story. He still owns earth's title deed and steers history to predetermined outcomes, but rebel occupiers have rejected his authority, seized the stage and are now largely running the show down here as *they* see fit. *"The whole world is under the control of the evil one"* (1 John 5:19b).

We need Jesus to return with a heavenly army, dethrone his rivals, reverse the damage they've caused and enforce God's universal rule as king. He has promised to. But until then we can help to advance his kingdom by (1) calling on him to intervene powerfully wherever we notice he's needed, (2) generously sharing ourselves and our resources to promote the message of Jesus and (3) working hard to make life better for people who are struggling.

GOD'S WILL - *"May your will be done, on earth as it is in heaven"* (v. 10b)

The fact that Jesus had to strain so intensely to accomplish the will of God should tell you something about what to expect as his apprentice. You can count on him, your Lord, to ask some hard things that you won't initially feel like doing. He will occasionally press you to change or discontinue some things that you enjoy and feel attached to. So this part of the prayer expresses an attitude you will repeatedly need to adopt if you mean to follow him.

OUR NEEDS - *"Give us today our daily bread"* (v. 11)

We are all dependent on God for more than we may think: a sound mind, decent health, restful sleep, emotional resilience, more patience, wisdom for good decisions, another chance, people who care, renewed resolve, success at what we attempt, steady work, enough cash, strength to endure, etc. Like bread, these are all essentials. But none of them is *always* available or securely in our grasp. And since fretting over them is both faithless and useless, Jesus recommends that we routinely look to God for what we need to make it through today and live it well for him.

OUR WRONGS - *"And forgive us our debts, as we also have forgiven our debtors"* (v. 12)

God sees our bad behaviors and unloving attitudes with far more sensitive eyes and a purer heart than ours. He understands that we are only dust, but we can still grieve him. As our surrogate, Jesus suffered the consequences our sins deserve, so they no longer block our access to God. But they *can* interfere with our freedom to enjoy and fellowship with him. If your heart feels uneasy in his presence or something seems "off" when you pray, do these two things right away: (1) Ask him to reveal and forgive any sins you haven't yet confessed. (2) Finish forgiving everyone who has hurt or wronged you.

> [14] For if you forgive other people when they sin against you, your heavenly Father will also forgive you. [15] But if you do not forgive others their sins, your Father will not forgive your sins. (Matthew 6:14–15)

OUR SAFETY - *"And lead us not into temptation, but deliver us from the evil one"* (v. 13)

One mark of wisdom is knowing when you need help and not hesitating to ask for it. It's especially important when you live every day as an exposed target in a world at war infested with ruthless enemies that you cannot see.[15] They are constantly plotting to cloud your mind, wound your heart, rob your peace, wear you down, light your fuse, blow things up, break your ties, crush your hope, shut your mouth, make you trip and take you out. To believe you are safe just because you don't *sense* danger is to play the fool. Even when everything appears to be good, you need to remember what's going on behind the scenes and keep asking your powerful God to keep you safe and steer you away from ambushes.

"For yours is the kingdom, and the power and the glory forever. Amen."

A well-meaning copyist added that conclusion to the Lord's Prayer many years after Matthew finished his gospel. Jesus himself didn't include an ending, so we don't need to either. Besides, it's better to think of prayer as something that never concludes, an ongoing conversation on a long trip with a close friend who is always in the seat right beside you.

Pray in the Spirit on all occasions with all kinds of prayers and requests. (Ephesians 6:18)

16 Rejoice always, 17 pray continually, 18 give thanks in all circumstances; for this is God's will for you in Christ Jesus. (1 Thessalonians 5:16–18)

EXERCISE: Imagine how much quality time you would spend with God if you met often to discuss each of the issues just described. He would love it and your world would change, starting with you. So here's an exercise you can practice to make it simpler in the times you set aside for God. As you answer each of the following questions, express your responses in a conversation with him. Then repeat the process often until the topics become a natural part of your interactions.

Our Father in heaven...
What is meaningful or special to you about the eternal Creator being your Father?

Hallowed be your name...
What do you especially admire, appreciate or find wonderful about God?

May your kingdom come -
Where do you notice that God seems to be missing or badly needed, and what do you wish he would do there?

May your will be done, on earth as it is in heaven -
1. What does God want you to do or to change?
2. What do you need to accept or let go of?

Give us this day our daily bread -
What do you (and those you care about) need in order to get through today and live it well?

Forgive us our debts as we also have forgiven our debtors -
1. For what do you need God's forgiveness and haven't yet sought it?
2. Whom do you need to finish forgiving?

Lead us not into temptation, but deliver us from the evil one -
1. What kind of temptation/trouble do you need God to guide you through or protect you from?
2. What do you need to stop thinking, wanting or doing because it is spiritually dangerous or could hurt someone?

---

15 We are not fighting against flesh-and-blood enemies, but against evil rulers and authorities of the unseen world, against mighty powers in this dark world, and against evil spirits in the heavenly places. (Ephesians 6:12, NLT)

RECOMMENDATION: Did you notice the nine plural pronouns in Jesus's prayer? He clearly meant us to pray it with others—not just by reciting it, but in the expanded way described above. Try it!

Encountering God in Scripture

Along with praying, it's supremely valuable to read or listen to some of the Bible in your times with God. Remember, the men who penned it were not just recording their own ideas or opinions. The words they chose were "God-breathed," so we are actually listening to him when we read what they wrote. Jesus believed we can neither survive nor succeed in life without them.

> People do not live by bread alone, but by every word that comes from the mouth of God. (Matthew 4:4b)

> [4] (Jesus said,) "Remain in me, as I also remain in you. No branch can bear fruit by itself; it must remain in the vine. Neither can you bear fruit unless you remain in me. [5] I am the vine; you are the branches. If you remain in me and I in you, you will bear much fruit; apart from me you can do nothing. [6] If you do not remain in me, you are like a branch that is thrown away and withers; such branches are picked up, thrown into the fire and burned. [7] If you remain in me and my words remain in you, ask whatever you wish, and it will be done for you." (John 15:4–7)

Ever-relational, God wants to rescue us from the puny, caricatured deity of our own understanding so we can know him as he really is. He is formally introduced in the Bible's first sentence and illuminates his awesome self to us on nearly every page.

People sometimes wonder what God looks like. According to Scripture, the unambiguous answer is that he looks just like Jesus. That's precisely what he told his followers in John 14:9: *"Anyone who has seen me has seen the Father."* So, doesn't it make sense to carefully, regularly, and systematically read and listen to the writings that reveal him up-close and personal?

A great place to start is with one of the first three gospels at the beginning of the NT using an easy-to-understand translation like the *New Living Translation* or *New International Version.* (Others like the *English Standard Version* and *New King James Version* are also good, but you may find them too formal or difficult.) When you finish, read John's gospel and keep going through each subsequent book until you finish Revelation. Mix in some Psalms for variety along the way. Then go after Genesis, Exodus and other books that pique your interest.

As you begin each time of reading, ask God's Spirit to help you understand with an open heart, and don't end it before answering these three "KEY" questions:

1. What is God *like*?
2. What does God *want*?
3. How should I *respond*?

A FINAL THOUGHT- It's unfortunately easy to pray and read Scripture religiously, yet fail to connect with God or draw nearer to him. The point of these practices isn't to check-off chores on your list of responsibilities. It's to draw near and share your heart with someone you love and to respond enthusiastically as he does the same with you. Stay focused on doing that as you spend time with him, and he will draw you further and deeper into a transforming closeness with himself.

Now make a few decisions that will influence how fully you get to know God as he intends:

How many days each week (__), where (_____), at what time(s) (_____) and for how long (_____) will you plan to meet alone with God to pray and absorb his Word?

Which of the ideas and suggestions you just read about will you incorporate into your times with God?

What else will you do throughout each day to help you stay engaged with God?

SECTION TWO

Loving God by TRUSTING Him

Since **God's goodness** is the final standard and norm, **our "good-enough"** simply isn't.

CHAPTER 6
HOW TO GET RIGHT WITH GOD

> **Q1:** If you were to die tonight and God asked, "Why should I let you into heaven?", how do you think you would respond?

That simple question is a great diagnostic tool. There are only two possible ways to answer it, and they are hopelessly incompatible, so they cannot both be correct. Everyone is depending on one way or the other to make them acceptable to God and eligible to spend eternity with him.

The WRONG Way to Get Right

The first answer is offered by those who are counting on God to accept them because they are "basically good" people. Their thinking goes something like this:

> *"As long as I try my best to live morally, treat people right, make a positive contribution, fulfill my obligations and not do anything terrible, I should be fine."*

That's a common response and it sounds reasonable. But the Bible says it's based on a serious misunderstanding and *cannot* work. Here are two reasons why:

You Can't Be Perfect

You're only human! You know it and God knows it. None of us *always* does the right thing. We don't even *want* to.

Who can say, "I have kept my heart pure; I am clean and without sin?" (Proverbs 20:9)

¹⁰ ... There is no one righteous, not even one. ... ²³ Everyone has sinned; we all fall short of God's glorious standard. (Romans 3:10, 23)

Part of being human means we're inclined to disregard, disrespect and disobey our Creator. That doesn't mean we're altogether awful, but it has created a dreadful dilemma for both him and us.

God Can't Excuse Sin

He can't overlook it or leave it be, any more than we can ignore a spot of black mold inside our house, or a smudge of dog poop on our shoe, or even the tiniest drop of cyanide in our water bottle.

The pristine purity of God's goodness causes him to react violently against sin. He cannot tolerate it in his presence. It is evil, infectious and deadly, and he hates it more intensely than we imagine. Even the things we think of as lesser sins, he regards as offensive and repulsive. As long as any of it is left uncleansed within us, he cannot be at peace with us or allow us into his heaven. Because we'll *ruin* it. Since his goodness is the final standard and norm, our "good-enough" simply *isn't*.

Without holiness (purity) no one will see the Lord. (Hebrews 12:14b)

Your sins have cut you off from God. Because of them, he has turned away .... (Isaiah 59:2, NLT)

The wages of sin is death .... (Romans 6:23)

No one can ever be made right with God by doing what (his) law commands. The law simply shows us how sinful we are. (Romans 3:20, NLT).

You should feel really uneasy if your answer to this chapter's opening question mentions anything about virtuous things you've done, the kind of decent person you are, how well you treat others or some evil act that you never committed. It's not possible for you to earn God's approval by being as good (= "righteous") as he requires, so it's not the answer or solution he wants you to rely on. Give it up already!

But don't *you* give up. God has devised an alternative way for us to get right with him forever, and it has nothing to do with our performance or character.

The ONLY Way to Get Right

A group of people asked Jesus to get to the point and tell them God's bottom line on this topic.

"What must we do to do the works God requires?" (John 6:28)

In other words, "We want God to be pleased with us and we're willing to give him whatever he wants. *What does he want?*" Jesus's surprising reply was that he fundamentally requires only one thing.

"The work of God is this: to **believe in** *the one he has sent. [That is, Me.]*" (John 6:29)

When Jesus told people they needed to "believe in" him, he wasn't just asking them to accept his words as true. He was going after something more profound and personal that included both their beliefs *and* their behavior. What he wants is for us to *trust* him, to put our *faith* in him. It involves **(1) believing that** he is completely trustworthy and **(2) actively depending on** him as though he is.

Dramatize it like this. You're out on a stroll and come to a large house nearly engulfed in flames. No one else is around. A distraught child starts crying out for help from a second story window spewing smoke. She shouts to you that she's going to leave the window and find her way down the hall to the stairs. But you can see she'll never make it out that way, so you shout back, "No! You need to *jump to me!* I will catch you and you'll be safe. *Trust* me."

You're actually asking the girl to do several things:

- **Not trust** in her own escape plan, but abandon it.
- **Do trust** (have faith / believe in) you to do what you promised.
- **Act on** her faith by jumping out of the window into your arms.

That's a decent illustration of how God wants us to respond to the One he sent to save us. It is the only "work" we must do to escape the fire of his judgment and be safe with him forever.

For God so loved the world that he gave his one and only Son, that whoever **believes in** him shall not perish but have eternal life. (John 3:16)

... We know that a person is made right with God by **faith in** Jesus Christ, not by obeying (*God's*) law. And we have **believed in** Christ Jesus, so that we might be made right with God because of our **faith in** Christ, not because we have obeyed (*God's*) law. For no one will ever be made right with God by obeying (*his*) law." (Galatians 2:16a, NLT)

[8] It is by grace you have been saved, through **faith**—and this is not from yourselves, it is the gift of God—[9] not by works, so that no one can boast. (Ephesians 2:8–9)

[4] The wages a person receives for working shouldn't be regarded as a gift but an obligation; they have been earned and are therefore deserved. But a right standing with God isn't something we can ever earn by working for it. [5] Instead he bestows it as a gift on those who are ungodly and don't deserve it, simply because they have turned to him and **trusted** him for it. He regards their **faith** as all that's necessary to make them righteous in his sight. (Romans 4:4–5, Paraphrase)

The last verse literally says, "their faith is credited as righteousness." That is incredible! The simple act of trusting God to forgive us (because of Jesus's work on our behalf) makes us instantly innocent before our Judge and permanently ready to live in his heaven. *That's* what he wants to hear us say we're counting on.

Q2: What person do you trust, and why do you trust them?

Q3: How does your faith in them affect the ways you interact with them?

Q4: Whom do you distrust, and why don't you trust them?

Q5: How does your lack of faith in them affect the ways you interact with them?

CHAPTER 7
TRUSTING JESUS FOR *ETERNAL* LIFE

There are two necessities for which we need to trust Jesus: *eternal* life and *everyday* life. The first launches our relationship with God, the second keeps it afloat and moving in the right direction. First:

> The wages of sin is death, but the free gift of God is eternal life through Christ Jesus our Lord. (Romans 6:23)

> [11] This is what God has testified: He has given us eternal life, and this life is in his Son. [12] Whoever has the Son has life; whoever does not have God's Son does not have life. [13] I have written this to you who believe in the name of the Son of God, so that you may know you have eternal life. (1 John 5:11–13, NLT)

Who has eternal life? Whoever has God's Son.

Who has God's Son? Whoever "believes in" Jesus's name.

What does that **mean?**
- Jesus's "name" represents Jesus himself—who and what he truly is.
- "Believing in his name" means the same thing as "trusting" or "having faith in" him.
- As we've already said, that idea includes both (1) *believing* certain things *about* Jesus and (2) *responding* in certain ways *to* Jesus. Let's look at both of those, starting here with what we must *believe*, followed in the next chapter with how we must *respond*.

Ten of Faith's Essential Beliefs

Essential Beliefs #1-4: Jesus Is Who He Said He Was

> [23] Jesus said, "You are from below; I am from above. You belong to this world; I do not. [24] That is why I said that you will die in your sins; for unless you believe that I AM who I claim to be, you will die in your sins." (John 8:23–24, NLT)

Think back: who did he and the inspired biblical writers claim that he was?

1. **He was the Son of Man** = The Head and leader of the human race

2. **He was the Son of David / Messiah** = **Christ** = Earth's ultimate king and ruler

3. **He was the Son of God** = Conceived by the Holy Spirit; both fully divine and fully human

4. **He was God the Son** = Eternal, co-equal member of the triune God, incarnate on earth as Jesus[16]

Essential Beliefs #5-8: Jesus Finished What He Came to Do

The Bible trumpets four, heaven-and-earth shaking accomplishments:

5. He fully revealed God

No one has ever seen God, but the one and only Son, who is himself God and is in closest relationship with the Father, has made him known. (John 1:18)

(Jesus said to his disciples:) "Anyone who has seen me has seen the Father." (John 14:9b)

6. He lived a perfect life

If Jesus had ever broken a single one of God's commandments, he would have become as guilty as everyone else and unable to save either himself or others from God's punishment.

Whoever keeps (God's) whole law and yet stumbles at just one point is guilty of breaking all of it. (James 2:10)

That makes God's final assessment of Jesus all-important for all of us:

We do not have a high priest who is unable to empathize with our weaknesses, but we have one who has been tempted in every way, just as we are—yet he did not sin. (Hebrews 4:15)

Christ (was) a lamb without blemish or defect. (1 Peter 1:19b)

7. He fully paid for all our sins

That phrase has become so familiar that many fail to grasp its meaning. Jesus ended his suffering on the cross by announcing an astounding new reality.

"It is finished." (John 19:30b)

---

[16] Some people won't yet know about or fully comprehend all four of these "identities" when they first decide to "believe in" Jesus, but it's reasonable to assume that their "saving faith" will embrace them as true once they learn more about him.

It wasn't just that the ordeal of crucifixion was over, but that the full fury of God's devastating response to human evil had just been directed at Jesus. His experience of the anguished nightmare awaiting unforgiven humans was officially over. The debt we owe God was completely paid off.

> [4] We thought his troubles were a punishment from God, a punishment for his own sins! [5] But [no,] he was pierced for our rebellion, crushed for our sins. He was beaten so we could be whole. He was whipped so we could be healed. [6] All of us, like sheep, have strayed away. We have left God's paths to follow our own. Yet the LORD laid on him the sins of us all. (Isaiah 53:4b–6, NLT)

> The Son of Man did not come to be served, but to serve, and to give his life as a ransom for many. (Matthew 20:28)

> Our High Priest offered himself to God as a single sacrifice for sins, good for all time. (Hebrews 10:12a)

There are only two "just" ways for God to resolve his hatred of our sins:
> EITHER: Give us what we deserve by making **us** pay for them.
> OR: Give us **better** than we deserve by directing his wrath elsewhere.

The second option is what he did with Jesus on the cross, giving him the hell that our evil deserves. Bearing that judgment is what Jesus was finally finished with and what made it possible for God to offer us a pardon. And that's what dealt the fatal blow to our last and worst enemy.

8. He vanquished death

> God raised Jesus from the dead, freeing him from the agony of death, because it was impossible for death to keep its hold on him. (Acts 2:24)

He had done nothing to deserve it, so it was forced to release him. And as its conqueror, he is able to defeat it on our behalf as well. Death is still allowed to swallow us up, but like Jonah's big fish, it cannot keep us down. Eventually it will have to vomit us back out again when the Lord returns for us.

> (God's grace) has now been revealed through the appearing of our Savior, Christ Jesus, who has destroyed death and has brought life and immortality to light through the gospel. (2 Timothy 1:10)

> Jesus guaranteed that "a time is coming when all who are in their graves will hear (my) voice and come out..." (John 5:28b-29a)

> (Jesus said:) "My Father's will is that everyone who looks to the Son and believes (trusts) in him shall have eternal life, and I will raise him up at the last day."[17] (John 6:40)

Jesus finished everything he came to earth to do, therefore...

---

[17] Also see 1 Corinthians 15:50-55 and 1 Thessalonians 4:15-18.

Essential Beliefs #9-10: Two Eternally-Momentous Realities Were Established

Jesus Is God's Ultimate Solution for Our Needs

9. Jesus Was Forever Exalted as Lord

9 God exalted Jesus to the highest place and gave him the name that is above every name, 10 that at the name of Jesus every knee should bow, in heaven and on earth and under the earth, 11 and every tongue acknowledge that Jesus Christ is Lord, to the glory of God the Father. (Philippians 2:9–11)

10. Jesus Will Now Save Anyone Who Trusts Him

27 My sheep listen to my voice; I know them, and they follow me. 28 I give them eternal life, and they shall never perish; no one will snatch them out of my hand. (John 10:27–28)

12 . . . The same Lord is Lord of all and richly blesses all who call on him, 13 for everyone who calls on the name of the Lord will be saved. (Romans 10:12b–13)

CONCLUSION: There is a huge contrast between the two basic ways we can attempt to get right with God and ready for heaven.
1. Either we depend on what *we've* done to make us worthy = FAITH IN OURSELVES.
2. Or we depend on what *he's* done *for* us to make us worthy = FAITH IN JESUS.

*God has settled this forever. Now **we** need to.*

20 No one can ever be made right with God by doing what (his) law commands. The law simply shows us how sinful we are. 21 But now God has shown us a way to be made right with him without keeping the requirements of the law, as was promised in the writings of Moses and the prophets long ago. 22 We are made right with God by placing our faith in Jesus Christ. And this is true for everyone who believes, no matter who we are. (Romans 3:20–22, NLT)

Q6: Do you have trouble accepting or understanding any of the ideas in this chapter?

Q7: How difficult is it to accept that your sins were so serious that Jesus had to die for them?

Q8: Are you right with God right-now?

Q9: Do you need to re-write your answer to this section's opening question? If so, do it.

SUMMARY: The kind of faith that pleases God and makes us "right" first consists of **believing** certain things to be true about Jesus, ten of which we just covered. But we can't end with those, because we also know that true "faith/belief/trust in Jesus" consists of **responding** to him in certain ways.

Two of Faith's Essential Responses

The fact that every sin ever committed was paid for by Jesus does *not* mean everyone on earth is automatically pardoned. Many go to their graves without making peace with God. We need to think of his forgiveness as being deposited into an account that we are only allowed to access when we turn to Jesus and trust him for it.

And remember, God only honors the kind of faith that both **believes** certain things about him and **responds** in certain ways to him.

The first public sermon preached after Jesus's resurrection was sharp and clear as it could be.

> 36 (Peter said to the crowd,) "Let all Israel be assured of this: God has made this Jesus, whom you crucified, both Lord and Messiah." 37 When the people heard this, they were cut to the heart and said to Peter and the other apostles, "Brothers, what shall we do?" 38 Peter replied, "Repent and be baptized, every one of you, in the name of Jesus Christ for the forgiveness of your sins." (Acts 2:36–38)

That former coward of an apostle boldly identified two things people must do in order to satisfy God and receive his forgiveness: repent and be baptized. *Together*, they are how true faith responds to Jesus for eternal life.

Trusting Jesus = Repentance + Baptism

Essential Response #1: Repentance

- **Repentance Requires a Repudiation of Our Merit**

It decides to stop trying to *earn* or *deserve* God's acceptance, knowing that it's only given to those who trust in Jesus as described above. Paul expressed it like this:

> [7] Whatever [good things I was or did that] were gains to me I now consider loss for the sake of Christ. [8] What is more, I consider everything a loss because of the surpassing worth of knowing Christ Jesus my Lord, for whose sake I have lost all things. I consider them garbage, that I may gain Christ [9] and be found in him, not having a righteousness of my own that comes from [keeping] the law, but that which is through faith in Christ—the righteousness that comes from God on the basis of faith. (Philippians 3:7–9)

- **Repentance Also Requires a Renunciation of Our Sins**

It determines to live every day, as much as possible, by these and similar instructions:

> Consider yourself to be dead to sin but alive to God in Christ Jesus. (Romans 6:11)

> [22] ... With regard to your former way of life, ... put off your old self which is being corrupted by its deceitful desires; [23] ... be made new in the attitude of your (mind); [24] and ... put on the new self, created to be like God in true righteousness and holiness. (Ephesians 4:22–24)

> [5] Put to death...whatever belongs to your earthly nature: sexual immorality, impurity, lust, evil desires and greed, which is idolatry. [6] Because of these, the wrath of God is coming. [7] You used to walk in these ways, in the life you once lived. [8] But now you must also rid yourself of all such things as these: anger, rage, malice, slander, and filthy language from your lips. (Colossians 3:5–8)

Q10: Have you ever thoroughly repented in both of the two ways just described? If not, what's missing?

Essential Response #2: Baptism

Some think of baptism as a purely *physical* act, a ritual of being sprinkled, doused or dunked in water. But God views it more as a *symbolic* act that portrays and declares two spiritual realities:

- ### An Expression of Confidence in God's Cleansing

It illustrates our desire and readiness for God to give us the ultimate spiritual bath and to purify us from everything that has defiled us.

> Now what are you waiting for? Get up, be baptized and wash your sins away, calling on Jesus's name. (Acts 22:16)

- ### A Participation in Jesus's Death and Resurrection

> [1] Well then, should we keep on sinning so that God can show us more and more of his wonderful grace? [2] Of course not! Since we have died to sin, how can we continue to live in it? [3] Or have you forgotten that when we were joined with Christ Jesus in baptism, we joined him in his death? [4] For we died and were buried with Christ by baptism. And just as Christ was raised from the dead by the glorious power of the Father, now we also may live new lives. (Romans 6:1–4)

Baptism symbolizes our sharing in Jesus's experience of "dying to" (being done and finished forever with) sin, then being resurrected to live forever-after for God. Obviously it doesn't mean you'll never sin again, but it does mean you don't *intend* to and will promptly *address* it when you realize that you have. In essence it means you are ready to...

> [13] ... Give yourself completely to God, for you were dead, but now you have new life. So use your whole body as an instrument to do what is right for the glory of God. [14] Sin is no longer your master, for you no longer live under the requirements of the law. Instead, you live under the freedom of God's grace. (Romans 6:13b–14, NLT)

Photo by Farinaz Athari

A good wedding is a great analogy. The centerpiece of the ceremony is when the bride and groom promise to love and be faithful to each other for better or worse, for richer or poorer, in sickness and in health, until death parts them. They are making sacred vows in the presence of God and witnesses to end ("die to") their lives as independent singles in order to live for each other from that moment on. They will fail to do so perfectly, but it still expresses their sincere intention, and God takes their vows seriously.

66

Q11: Have you been baptized to express your acceptance of the two things it portrays? [18]

Q12: If not, why not, and are you now ready to be?

---

[18] Some wonder if they should be re-baptized because they already received it as infants or children. Or they chose to do it later but didn't fully understand what they were doing. Or they wandered from their faith and want to sincerely re-commit themselves to following Jesus from now on. Since biblical baptism is loaded with meaning, it makes sense to do it again if you were too young to comprehend it. But if you *did* understand and simply weren't faithful to the Lord as you intended, you don't need to be re-baptized any more than a lousy spouse needs to restart their marriage with a second wedding. What's needed is repentance and a reaffirmation of your original faith and devotion.

SUPPLEMENT C – CAN WE LOSE IT ONCE WE GET IT?

All this talk about depending on Jesus for eternal life surfaces a few follow-up questions:

- *Once I repent and trust in him, is the "salvation" I receive <u>permanent</u>? Or can I possibly lose it through some spiritual blowout or neglect?*

- *How confident can I be that I'm now reconciled with God and headed for heaven? How entitled am I to believe that I will remain "eternally secure" in my relationship with him?*

The NT responds to these from two angles for the sake of balance. The verses referenced are full of rich ideas and are worth reading if the questions are weighing on you or someone you care about.

1. Assurance – True Christians are encouraged to rejoice that they are now-and-forever accepted by God and welcome in his heavenly kingdom.

- He has forgiven all their past, present and future sins, so they will never be condemned. (Colossians 2:13–14; Romans 5:1, 9; 8:1; Hebrews 10:11–18; 1 John 2:1–2)

- He has given them eternal, unending life. (John 5:24; 6:39–40; 11:25–26; 1 John 5:11–13)

- He has formally adopted them into his family. (John 1:12–13; Romans 8:15; Ephesians 1:5)

- He has given them his Holy Spirit as a "down payment" and guarantee of their final inheritance. (Ephesians 5:13–14; 1 Peter 1:3–4)

- Jesus has promised to return and take them to live in the place he prepared for them in his Father's house. (John 14:1–3)

- Until the day Jesus returns, he will carry on to completion the good work he began within them. (Philippians 1:6)

- God's protective hold on them is as unbreakable as he is powerful. (John 10:28–29)

2. Caution – The problem with those assurances is that they only apply to "true Christians," and it isn't always obvious who they are. Some people *think* they are (and may appear so to others), but in God's reality they *aren't*. Think of Judas Iscariot for over three years! No one but Jesus knew his heart until after his betrayal, and his wasn't an isolated case of mistaken identity. Hypocrisy and self-delusion are common. That's why Jesus warns:

> [21] "Not everyone who calls out to me, 'Lord! Lord!' will enter the Kingdom of Heaven. Only those who actually do the will of my Father in heaven will enter. [22] On judgment day many will say to me, 'Lord! Lord! We prophesied in your name and cast out demons in your name and performed many miracles in your name.' [23] But I will reply, 'I never knew you. Get away from me, you who break God's laws.'" (Matthew 7:21-23, NLT; also see 2 Corinthians 11:15 and 1 John 2:18–19)

The flip-side is that it's also possible for us to doubt we are true Christians because of some haunting flaw or breakdown, but in God's reality we *are*. Think how Peter must have felt after he repeatedly ranted and swore up-and-down that he didn't even *know* Jesus (in Matthew 26:69–74). But slumps are not the same as apostasy. The grace of God ensured that Peter's horrific fail ended up as only a blip on a normally-stellar, God-honoring record.

So the better question is not if we can *lose* our salvation, but if we ever really *had* it in the first place. Jesus said we can (usually) know if someone is his by "checking their fruit" (Matthew 7:16–20). Paul sharpened that idea into an imperative:

Examine yourselves to see whether you are in the faith; test yourselves. (2 Corinthians 13:5)

We all exhibit "tells" that indicate the presence or absence of genuine faith within us, so Scripture tells us to check ourselves for these particular...

Signs of Spiritual Life:

- Do you believe that Jesus is the Messiah-King, God's perfect son sent to pay the debt for your sins? (1 John 2:1–2; 22-25; 4:15)

- Do you also believe that Jesus was physically resurrected from death and now rules as Lord over all? (1 Corinthians 15:14, 17; Romans 10:9; Philippians 2:9–11)

- Do you believe that Jesus has made you right with God by providing you with his forgiveness and eternal life? (Romans 5:1–2; 1 John 5:9-13)

- Do you regularly seek to love God most and spend quality time with him in his Word, prayer and at church? (John 15:4-7; 1 John 2:15-19)

- Do you sincerely desire to please God and live every part of your life according to his word? (1 John 1:5–7; 2:3–6, 29; 3:2–10)

- Are you usually willing to admit and repent of your sins? (1 John 1:8–9)

- Do you strive to resolve your resentments and forgive people who hurt or wrong you? (1 John 2:9–11; 3:14–15)

- Do you frequently show love for others by seeking to help and bless them? (1 John 3:16–23; 4:7–12; Matthew 25:31–46)

- Do you often look for ways to serve/represent the Lord and "bear fruit?" (John 15:1–6)

- Are you determined to remain devoted and loyal to Jesus for all the days of your life? (Matthew 10:22; Colossians 1:22-23; Hebrews 3:14; 6:10-12; James 1:12; Revelation 2:10)

You probably guessed that the best answer to all those questions is **Yes**! At least *mostly*. If you can say that in good conscience, God invites you to confidently claim all of his rock-solid assurances as your own.

If you *can't*, you may have reason to doubt that you are "saved" or a true Christian as the Bible defines one. Maybe you never were. You *might* simply be in a slump or temporarily adrift. But perhaps you never possessed the kind of informed and submissive trust God is after. That could be so even if you grew up in a faith-filled home, prayed a certain prayer, "invited Jesus into your heart," liked church, lived a good life and sometimes feel close to God.

If you're not certain, the remedy to your current condition is as straightforward as the contents of this chapter. Turn your attention toward God, admit (and offer a sincere apology for) your sins, ask him to forgive you, and express your readiness to live for him from now on as best you can. Then thank him warmly for responding to you, and get on with it. The rest of this course will help.

CHAPTER 8
TRUSTING JESUS IN *EVERYDAY* LIFE

*B*eing a Christian means little more to some folks than "getting saved" by "asking Jesus into their heart" and going to heaven after they die. It's a shallow, short-sighted version of what God has in mind. Trusting Jesus for eternal life walks most of us to the starting line of a marathon race during which we will need to trust Jesus every day, partly because of four pungent realities.

Reality #1: Life On Earth Is Sometimes Awful

Sometimes it still surprises me that God doesn't protect his children from as many problems or difficulties ("trials") as he could. Even his "favorites" frequently have to struggle with things like...

- **Painful circumstances** in the form of bad news, poor health, financial setbacks, heavy pressure, natural disasters, relationship breakdowns and so forth.

- **Difficult people** who are insensitive, rude, uncaring, impatient, self-absorbed, mean, abusive, violent, disloyal and other unkind things.

- **Internal struggles** with anxiety and fear, anger and resentment, addiction, selfishness and sin, guilt and remorse, sadness and grief, loss and loneliness, mental illness, pain, etc.

Q13: What have you recently experienced that qualifies as a "trial"?

The filter God uses to screen our troubles turns out to have some king-size holes in it. Why is that? The Almighty is our Father, so why doesn't he protect us better? *"Why?"* is the question that vexes and injures more people's faith than any other. So we also need to understand these next few realities.

Reality #2: God Has Promised to End All Evil

The reason the Son of God appeared was to destroy the devil's work. (1 John 3:8b)

He hates it more than we do. Not only because evil and injustice are intrinsically grotesque, but because he loves us and wants us to be happy. Just as we do for *our* children!

Scripture assures us that he has already initiated a comprehensive, two-stage plan to purge the world of evil. On "the Day of the Lord" at the end of this age, Jesus will return as the Commander of heaven's vast army to forcefully take charge of everything.[19] But that's the *second* stage of his plan. Until then...

Reality #3: God Allows (Some) Evil to Exist – It doesn't seem to make sense why he would until we remember his primary reason for creating us in the first place:

He Wants Those He Loves to Love Him Back

That has been his heart's desire since he designed the first humans. But **Love Requires Freedom**. It isn't love if it isn't freely chosen or it's programmed-in. For people (and other beings) to truly love God, they must have the ability *not* to. Robots and AI can't because they don't. But once we possess it, **Freedom Can Choose Evil**.

Adam and Eve turned their backs on Love and exercised their God-given freedom by setting aside his prohibition in favor of an option that seemed better at the moment. They breached a protective dam that released a torrent of spiritual sewage into the world, fatally poisoning them, their relationship with God, their home, and all their heirs. And now, thousands of years downstream, the result is that our planet is saturated with evil like a body with Stage Four cancer. Terrible things go on down here all the time.

And what do we wish God would *do* about it? *Intervene!* Step in and fix it! At least prevent it from becoming worse. Stop the perpetrators of evil before they can act. A few targeted lightning bolts or heart attacks would be a fine start.

But where would God stop that kind of intervention once he started? Certainly he'd take out the worst-of-the-worst: the child molesters, sex-traffickers, terrorists, drug lords, rapists and murderers. But what about the thieves, scammers, cheaters and mean drunks? Or the complainers, gossips, trolls, reckless drivers, hurtful parents, addicts, liars and spitters?

If tonight God started scrubbing the world clean of all evil, would any of us still be here for tomorrow's breakfast? I'm sure *I* wouldn't. The problem is that ...

---

[19] Joel 2:11; Isaiah 25:6-9; Revelation 19:11-16; 21:1-22:5

Some Degree of Evil Exists Inside Us All

We talked about this earlier. Some people are obviously better than others, but none of us are as good as God.

> *The line separating good and evil passes not through states, nor between classes, nor between political parties either—but right through every human heart—and through all human hearts. This line shifts. Inside us, it oscillates with the years. ...Even in the best of all hearts, there remains an un-uprooted small corner of evil.* (Aleksandr Solzhenitsyn, The Gulag Archipelago, Volume 2, pages 5–6)

To some degree each of us contributes to evil's persistence in our world. Once God starts uprooting and destroying all of it, that will be the end of everyone with whom he hasn't reconciled. But he's not yet ready for that.

> The Lord is not slow in keeping his promise, as some understand slowness. Instead he is being patient with (us), not wanting anyone to perish, but everyone to come to repentance. (2 Peter 3:9)

The soul of his right-now, *first-stage* strategy is to focus on us one at a time and renovate us to become more like Jesus. As he shrinks the tumors of evil within us as individuals, we can then become part of his solution to the *world's* evil instead of making it worse.[20] But for that plan to succeed while other forces strive to overpower us, our faith will need to become more resilient and dominant. That brings us to a fourth reality we need to recognize in order to respond as he desires.

Reality #4: Our Faith Is Supremely Valuable

> [7] Blessed are those who trust in the LORD and have made the LORD their hope and confidence. [8] They are like trees planted along a riverbank, with roots that reach deep into the water. Such trees are not bothered by the heat or worried by long months of drought. Their leaves stay green, and they never stop producing fruit. (Jeremiah 17:7–8, NLT)

> [6] Be truly glad. There is wonderful joy ahead, even though now you must endure many trials for a little while. [7] These trials will show that your faith is genuine. It is being tested as fire tests and purifies gold—though your faith is far more precious than mere gold. So when your faith remains strong through many trials, it will bring you much praise and glory and honor on the day when Jesus Christ is revealed to the whole world. (1 Peter 1:6–7, NLT)

It may not *seem* to matter much, but God is enormously pleased when you continue to trust him while you're baffled or struggling or hurting. He is honored by your steady confidence. And once it has been purified and strengthened even more, your faith will become more precious to him than pure gold is to you. In fact, a day is coming when he will publicly recognize and *cheer* you for it.

---

[20] That's what the sections in this book on Serving Him and Loving Others are going to cover.

The condition of a person's faith can often be read by their responses to danger, pain, setbacks, frustrations, mistreatment, temptations, and failure, especially when they're prolonged.

CHAPTER 9
GOD IS DEVOTED TO IMPROVING OUR FAITH

I quit going to the gym during the two years when COVID was ravaging the planet. Then I stalled for a couple more years because I prefer to sit and talk or read rather than work out. Every trace of my once-defined upper body vanished and was replaced by a sad softness and strain whenever I lifted anything heavier than a jar of almond butter.

Sort of like that, most people's faith is like a weak and flabby muscle. That explains why so many of us quickly lose our composure when life gets disagreeable. It's also why God is determined to exercise and strengthen it over time. Here's a simplified explanation of how he goes about it.

> [2] Dear brothers and sisters, when troubles *(trials)* of any kind come your way, consider it an opportunity for great joy. [3] For you know that when your faith is tested, your endurance has a chance to grow. [4] So let it grow, for when your endurance is fully developed, you will be perfect and complete, needing nothing. (James 1:2–4, NLT)

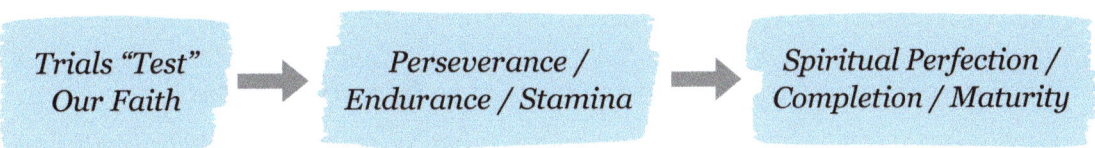

Some Truth about Trials

1. They are difficult and unpleasant, but it's *possible* to view them as strategic opportunities to become spiritually fit and close to God.

2. They come to us in a wide variety of forms, typically as people, places and things that displease us in some way.

3. They are inevitable no matter how much we try to avoid them. James 1:2 says *when*, not *if*, trials come our way. If you're in a phase where everything is going well, be grateful and enjoy it. But don't expect it to last indefinitely. People who believe God has promised them perpetual health, happiness and success have badly misunderstood his timing and ways. Jesus summarized it like this:

"In this world you will have trouble. But take heart! I have overcome the world [and will walk with you through it]" (John 16:33b).

4. They can be dangerous. The word "trial" can just as well be translated "temptation," referring to anything that entices us to doubt God or respond poorly.

5. They play a crucial role in our growth and relationship with God.

   - They reveal the true nature of our faith by challenging it. They force us to re-decide if we fully trust God and to respond accordingly.

   - If we *do* decide that, our faith becomes more resolute and confident, more sturdy and dependable, like the muscle strength and stamina that result from regular, strenuous exercise.

   - As our faith develops, our entire character is transformed and we become more like Jesus in how we handle the difficulties and challenges we encounter.

   - So it actually makes sense why James would tell us to welcome and relish our trials instead of hating and chafing against them. They prompt us to mature and toughen into Christlike people who are good at life and excel at demonstrating our love for God by trusting him. If that's what you truly want, this is really good news.[21] Notice how Paul welcomed it after wrestling with a malady of his own.

[7b] In order to keep me from becoming conceited [after receiving a vision of heaven], I was given a thorn in my flesh, a messenger of Satan, to torment me. [8] Three times I pleaded with the Lord to take it away from me. [9] But he said to me, "My grace is sufficient for you, for my power is made perfect in weakness." Therefore I will boast all the more gladly about my weaknesses, so that Christ's power may rest on me. [10] That is why, for Christ's sake, I delight in weaknesses, in insults, in hardships, in persecutions, in difficulties. For when I am weak, then I am strong. (1 Corinthians 12:7b–10)

Q14: What made Paul able to respond to his trial as he eventually did?

Q15: What is your honest response to knowing that God regularly tests you and employs trials to help you grow?

---

[21] We'll look more at this in the coming section on "Delighting in the Lord" in negative circumstances.

Q16: Describe another trial you recently experienced that is different from the one you identified in your answer to Q13.

Q17: How would you describe your reactions and responses to those two trials?

The Bible contains vivid illustrations of faith being tested that are loaded with useful insights. Here's a great one:

> [35] As evening came, Jesus said to his disciples, "Let's cross to the other side of the lake." [36] So they took Jesus in the boat and started out, leaving the crowds behind (although other boats followed). [37] But soon a fierce storm came up. High waves were breaking into the boat, and it began to fill with water. [38] Jesus was sleeping at the back of the boat with his head on a cushion. The disciples woke him up, shouting, "Teacher, don't you care that we're going to drown?" [39] When Jesus woke up, he rebuked the wind and said to the waves, "Silence! Be still!" Suddenly the wind stopped, and there was a great calm. [40] Then he asked them, "Why are you afraid? Do you still have no faith?" [41] They were terrified and asked each other, "Who is this? Even the wind and the waves obey him!" (Mark 4:35–41)

Allow me to add a few observations and a dumb question.

- Crossing the lake (the "Sea of Galilee") was a normal occurrence at the time. The disciples were simply doing what they were told and everything seemed fine.

- That lake was about 13 miles long and eight miles wide, so they were planning on a few hours for their trip.

- After a while the weather grew increasingly unfriendly and started to feel dangerous. Their boat was getting violently tossed about and the men couldn't bail fast enough to keep the water where it belonged.

- The situation soon became dire. It realistically looked as though a disaster was about to occur. *(Perhaps as it did in the two trials you wrote about, above.)*

- *Where was God?* There was no sign of him and no way to escape.

Q18: How did Jesus assess the disciples' faith in response to that test, and why?

Jesus sounded pretty disappointed with them; it wasn't the kind of response he was looking for. He could *tell* they lacked faith simply by observing their reactions.

Q19: What could the disciples have said and done differently to display a more commendable faith in that situation? *Write two or three answers, and be specific.*

Here's what I'm getting at. We can often read the condition of a person's faith by how they respond to danger, difficulty, pain, setbacks, disappointment, confusion, loss, bad news, provocations, mistreatment, temptations, and failure, especially when they're prolonged.

We can also improve the quality of our faith by responding to them more often as God desires. We just need to learn how, so understanding the following will help.

CHAPTER 10
SOME STANDOUT QUALITIES OF ROBUST FAITH

The kind of faith that God deserves and keeps us steady expresses itself in several smart and predictable ways when it's being tested.

1. It Doesn't Panic

Lingering fear, worry and anxiety often[22] indicate that our faith is faltering, like warning lights on a car's dashboard alerting us to pay attention and take action. I may be faintly overstating it, but Scripture presents faith as God's standard antidote to all of those agitators. It renders them nearly powerless, and it works equally well to dissolve any feelings of resentment toward God.

2. It's Quick to Involve God

A life-threatening storm may not appear dangerous in its initial stage. That would explain why the disciples responded as they did when the weather started acting up. But as it became more intense, they continued *not* to rouse Jesus until their boat was close to sinking. God's miracle-working Agent was right there within earshot the whole time! Why did they wait so long to involve him?

Probably for the same reasons we do. We're not normally inclined to think of him right away when faced with demanding circumstances or people. They don't always feel like a big deal at first. And even when they do, we usually just try to handle them because we believe we can.

The problem is that prolonging the delay before we reach out to God gives our trials longer to intensify and provoke stronger reactions within us. It's better to turn to God sooner rather than later. Don't just sit there and fret over what's going on or about to happen. Wake him up!

God is our refuge and strength, always ready to help in times of trouble. (Psalm 46:1, NLT)

You do not have because you do not ask God. (James 4:2c)

---

[22] Often, but not always. Panic can also be triggered by underlying mental health, brain chemistry and/or physical issues which cannot usually be cured by faith alone.

Here's a good place to start when you don't know how to think or respond to what's happening:

> If any of you lacks wisdom, you should ask God, who gives generously to all without finding fault, and it will be given to you.[23] (James 1:5)

I've taken that advice more times than I can count, usually when I'm agitated or starting to react impulsively. I've honestly been amazed by how often—and how quickly—I "become aware" of a fresh insight or alternate perspective that calms me down and clarifies my next step. *(More on this in a moment.)* Often it comes in the form of seeing how I'm contributing to the problem. But simple wisdom isn't always all we lack, so Scripture also tells us to involve him like this:

> Cast all your anxiety on him because he cares for you. (1 Peter 5:7)

Tell him how you feel and what you need. For Jesus's disciples in the boat, faith-prompted prayers might have sounded something like: "Lord, it's getting ominous out here and we're starting to feel overwhelmed. This looks like one of those times when we need you to handle a thing that's too big for us. We know you can manage it and we're eager to see what you're going to do; we're just wondering what you have in mind. Would you please _____? Is there anything you want from *us*?" Or maybe something like this would feel more authentic for you:

> [1] How long, LORD? Will you forget me forever? How long will you hide your face from me? [2] How long must I wrestle with my thoughts and day after day have sorrow in my heart? How long will my enemy triumph over me? [3a] Look on me and answer, LORD my God. Give light to my eyes, or I will sleep in death. (Psalm 13:1–3a)[24]

3. It Rehearses the Truth

> [31] Jesus said, "If you hold to my teaching, you are really my disciples. [32] Then you will know the truth, and the truth will set you free." (John 8:31–32)

Difficult situations and interactions conjure-up mistaken, inflammatory, even irrational ideas in our minds about what's happening. They manipulate us into questioning or forgetting what we normally believe to be true and so lead us to react poorly. They cause us to lose sight of Jesus.[25]

Q20: **What are some basic truths about God that Jesus's disciples doubted or forgot as the storm thrashed and threatened to sink them?**

---

[23] Wisdom includes seeing situations and people as God does, from his point of view, and understanding the best ways to respond to them.

[24] The 150-chapter book of *Psalms* provides many such examples of how faith prays.

[25] The classic illustration of this is Peter's experience of *not* walking on water for very long in Matthew 14:22–31.

POSSIBLE ANSWERS:

- *He knows what we're going through and it fits perfectly into his plans for us.*
- *He uses trials just like this to challenge and develop our faith.*
- *He's right here with us to help us get through this.*
- *No one dies until God says it's their time.*
- *Whatever happens, even if we have to suffer for a while, we're going to be okay.*

> *God's preferred way to bolster our faith is not to fix our problem but to correct **our** perspective by informing us of **his**.*

Relevant, biblically-factual statements like the ones you just read provide us with "wisdom" and act like internal gyroscopes to keep us emotionally and spiritually stable. Thus he protects us from being wrecked by every strong storm that blows our way.

For example: My parents died within a year of each other in 2018. They were both smart, fun, popular, dear to me and firmly agnostic regarding God. Though we discussed spiritual things numerous times over 45 years, neither of them ever showed much interest or concern. They may have had eternity-altering deathbed conversions, but not as far I know.

How can that *not* unsettle my faith and fill me with dread when I think about their current condition and ultimate fate? Only by remembering and clinging to what the Bible assures me is true about God, both now and forever.

Righteousness and justice are the foundation of (his) throne. (Psalms 89:14)

Far be it from (God) …to treat the righteous and the wicked alike. Far be it from you! Will not the Judge of all the earth do right? (Genesis 18:25)

Of course he will! He *cannot* do otherwise. He *must* take everything into consideration and be absolutely fair with every individual, because he is entirely and inflexibly *Good*. No one will ever be rejected or sent to hell by mistake. When I go to be with him and can see things more as he does, I'm confident I will 100% approve and appreciate him for all his decisions. Because I know the truth about him, I don't have to worry about my parents—or anything else, for that matter.

That's the basic response God advocates whenever our faith gets challenged or assaulted. Focus again on what's true from his point of view, even if you're not *feeling* it. Affirm it repeatedly and forcefully as though you're fighting drowsiness on a lengthy drive and can't afford to doze.

Finally, brothers and sisters, whatever is true, whatever is noble, whatever is right, whatever is pure, whatever is lovely, whatever is admirable—if anything is excellent or praiseworthy—think about (*ponder*) such things. (Philippians 4:8)

EXERCISE: Read slowly and reflectively what the following verses (in Supplement D) tell us to remember and cling to when we're under siege or "in over our heads." Highlight the ones you most need to remember.

SUPPLEMENT D - FACE THESE FACTS WHEN GRAPPLING WITH TRIALS

God's Loyalty and Devotion

[1] ... Listen to the LORD who created you: "Do not be afraid, for I have ransomed you. I have called you by name; you are mine. [2] When you go through deep waters, I will be with you. When you go through rivers of difficulty, you will not drown. When you walk through the fire of oppression, you will not be burned up; the flames will not consume you. [3a] For I am the LORD, your God, the Holy One of Israel, your Savior... [4b] You are precious to me. You are honored, and I love you." (Isaiah 43:1–4b, NLT)

God has said, "Never will I leave you; never will I forsake you." (Hebrews 13:5b)

[4] (Therefore,) even when I walk through the darkest valley, I will not be afraid, for you are close beside me. Your rod and your staff protect and comfort me. ... [6] Surely your goodness and unfailing love will pursue me all the days of my life, and I will live in the house of the LORD forever. (Psalm 23:4, 6, NLT)

God's Ingenuity and Power

[28] We know that God causes everything to work together for the good of those who love God and are called according to his purpose for them. [29a] For ... he chose them to become like his Son.... (Romans 8:28–29a, NLT)

"I am the LORD, the God of all mankind. Is anything too hard for me?" (Jeremiah 32:27)

God's Protection

[27] "My sheep listen to my voice; I know them, and they follow me. [28] I give them eternal life, and they shall never perish; no one will snatch them out of my hand. [29] My Father, who has given them to me, is greater than all; no one can snatch them out of my Father's hand. [30] I and the Father are one." (John 10:27–30)

God's Kindness and Understanding

[8] The LORD is compassionate and gracious, slow to anger, abounding in love. [9] He will not always accuse, nor will he harbor his anger forever; [10] he does not treat us as our sins deserve or repay us according to our iniquities. [11] For as high as the heavens are above the earth, so great is his love for those who fear him; [12] as far as the east is from the west, so far has he removed our transgressions from us. [13] As a father has compassion on his children, so the LORD has compassion on those who fear him; [14] for he knows how we are formed, he remembers that we are dust. (Psalm 103:8–14)

God's Assistance

[26] The Spirit helps us in our weakness. We do not know what we ought to pray for, but the Spirit himself intercedes for us through wordless groans. [27] And he who searches our hearts knows the mind of the Spirit, because the Spirit intercedes for God's people in accordance with the will of God. (Romans 8:26–27)

The God of all grace, who called you to his eternal glory in Christ, after you have suffered a little while, will himself restore you and make you strong, firm and steadfast. (1 Peter 5:10)

The temptations [and trials] in your life are no different from what others experience. And God is faithful. He will not allow the temptation (trial) to be more than you can stand. When you are tempted (tried), he will show you a way out so that you can endure. (1 Corinthians 10:13, NLT)

God's Love and Mercy

[21] I still dare to hope when I remember this: [22] The faithful love of the LORD never ends! his mercies never cease. [23] Great is his faithfulness; his mercies begin afresh each morning. (Lamentations 3:21)

[38] I am convinced that (nothing) ... [39] in all creation will be able to separate us from the love of God that is in Christ Jesus our Lord. (Romans 8:38–39, NLT)

God's Forgiveness

[5] [Jesus] was pierced for our rebellion, crushed for our sins. He was beaten so we could be whole. He was whipped so we could be healed. [6] All of us, like sheep, have strayed away. We have left God's paths to follow our own. Yet the LORD laid on him the sins of us all. (Isaiah 53:5–6)

So now there is no condemnation for those who belong to Christ Jesus. (Romans 8:1)

If we confess our sins, he is faithful and just (to) forgive us our sins and purify us from all unrighteousness. (1 John 1:9)

God's Expectations and Promise

[34] "Do not suppose that I have come to bring peace to the earth. I did not come to bring peace, but a sword. ... [36] A man's enemies will be the members of his own household. [37] Anyone who loves their father or mother more than me is not worthy of me; anyone who loves their son or daughter more than me is not worthy of me. [38] Whoever does not take up their cross and follow me is not worthy of me. [39] Whoever finds their life will lose it, and whoever loses their life for my sake will find it." (Matthew 10:34–39)

"Don't be afraid of what you are about to suffer. ... If you remain faithful even when facing death, I will give you the crown of life." (Revelation 2:10)

Sometimes a good song is the best way to embed an encouraging truth into your soul. Here are a few uplifting recommendations you can add to your list of favorites.

- *It Is Well with My Soul*, written by Horatio Spafford in 1873 after his four children drowned

- *Even If*, by Mercy Me

- *Praise You in This Storm*, by Casting Crowns

- *Blessed Be Your Name*, by Tree63; based on Job's famous words after tragedy struck

Robust faith interrupts the mutterings of doubt, resentment and anxiety in our hearts. Paul says in Ephesians 6:16 that faith works like a Roman soldier's shield to deflect and quench our enemy's flaming arrows. It refuses to badmouth God or throw up its hands in despair and assume the worst. It resists being swept-up by the mood of the moment or the opinions of others, and it speaks-up to remind us of what we know to be true—what God swears is true in his Word.

"Faith remembers in the dark what we learned in the light."

Another standout quality of commendable faith is that...

4. It Gives Thanks

> [6] Do not be anxious about anything, but in every situation, by prayer and petition, with thanksgiving, present your requests to God. [7] And the peace of God, which transcends all understanding, will guard your heart and your mind in Christ Jesus. (Philippians 4:6–7)

Right there in verse 6, hiding in plain sight, is one of the most powerful and heartening "secrets" in the Bible. It is a veritable antidote for anxiety. God-honoring faith doesn't merely offer bare prayers; it also expresses *gratitude*.[24]

We usually thank a person for what they've done *after* they do it. But here it tells us to thank him *before* he does it. Why so?

Because giving thanks expresses our faith in the God we're petitioning. It's a way of telling him we trust him to respond and we know he's got us covered, even if we still *feel* afraid or upset. This is one of the keys to growing a more intimate and solid relationship with God. And something miraculous happens when we do it sincerely.

> (Then) the peace of God, which transcends all understanding, will guard your heart and your mind in Christ Jesus. (Philippians 4:7)

---

[24] What are we supposed to thank God *for*? The *New Living Translation* of verse 6 says we should "thank him for what he's done (in the past)." That can certainly be part of the idea, but limiting it to past events obscures a key insight. The biblical writer literally tells us to ask *"with thanksgiving,"* to thank God while we're still in the act of asking for what we need, when it doesn't yet appear that he's done anything at all.

> **Q22:** Which of your prayers has God not *yet* answered that you should thank him for *now*?

Next, how does faith express itself when we're not sure *how* God will respond to our requests?

5. It Submits to God

Imagine the dark scene in the Garden of Gethsemane where Jesus was agonizing over what he was about to face. The essence of his repeated prayer was:

> "Father, if you are willing, take this cup from me; yet not my will, but yours be done." (Luke 22:42)

The Bible encourages us to fervently and repeatedly request whatever is on our hearts when we pray, as Jesus did. But it doesn't guarantee that we will always experience relief or get rescued in this life. There are times when we simply need to relent and accept that what we're pursuing may not be God's will. What *we* want isn't necessarily what *he* wants. What should we do then?

Sometimes the answer is just to stop asking and leave the outcome in his competent hands, confident that he will do what's best. Faith isn't always "certainty" that he'll do exactly what you ask; it's confidence in God as a good Father and willingness to do whatever he tells you, even if it's hard.

> **Q23:** What do you need to accept, adapt to or make peace with "as it is"—at least for *now*?

6. It Persists

If God's answer to our prayer isn't a flat "No," it may instead be "Not like that," or "Not now." Any of those responses can trigger discouragement or frustration if we forget that he always, *always* responds as he does for wise and loving reasons. Sometimes we should keep asking, but other times we need to adjust our expectations and focus more on learning what he's trying to teach. The apostle Paul did, though apparently it took him a while to get good at it.

12b ... I have learned the secret of being content in any and every situation, whether well fed or hungry, whether living in plenty or in want. 13 I can do all this through him who gives me strength. (Philippians 4:12b–13) (*Compare this with 2 Corinthians 12:2-10, an amazing account of learning how to manage and flourish while in the midst of painful circumstances.*)

The One who sees and cares for us deserves to be trusted in every moment, including our worst and last. Turning to, depending on and waiting patiently for him to supply what we need when we're in trouble is one of the most loving ways our faith can express itself. Especially when his responses seem to be slooow.

My help comes from the LORD, the Maker of heaven and earth. (Psalm 121:2)

5 Yes, my soul, find rest in God; my hope comes from him. 6 Truly he is my rock and my salvation; he is my fortress, I will not be shaken. 7 My salvation and my honor depend on God; he is my mighty rock, my refuge. 8 Trust in him at all times, you people; pour out your hearts to him, for God is our refuge. (Psalm 62:5–8)

24 I say to myself, "The LORD is my inheritance; therefore, I will hope in him!" 25 The LORD is good to those who depend on him, to those who search for him. 26 So it is good to wait quietly for salvation from the LORD. (Lamentations 3:24)

13 I remain confident of this: I will see the goodness of the LORD in the land of the living. 14 Wait for the LORD; be strong and take heart and wait for the LORD. (Psalm 27:13–14)

12 Be careful, dear brothers and sisters. Make sure that your own hearts are not evil and unbelieving, turning you away from the living God. 13 You must warn each other every day, while it is still "today," so that none of you will be deceived by sin and hardened against God. 14 For if we are faithful to the end, trusting God just as firmly as when we first believed, we will share in all that belongs to Christ. (Hebrews 3:12–14, NLT)

"The one who stands firm to the end will be saved." (Matthew 24:13)

*How well you're doing spiritually—the overall condition of your relationship with God—largely depends on how persistently and decisively you trust him. It's also a fair measure of how well you **love** him.*

Q24: Think back to the trials you mentioned in your answers to Q13 and Q16. Pick one of the following four words that best describes your faith's response to each of those trials, and write it on the blank line, below: **Absent   Weak   Mixed   Strong**
Remember, faith's presence and absence express themselves both internally (in thoughts, feelings and attitudes) and externally (in words, reactions and behavior).

- My Faith During Trial #1: _____. Reasons for this assessment:

- My Faith During Trial #2: _____. Reasons for this assessment:

Q25: Which of these six qualities was on display or missing-in-action during the worst of your two trials?

1. It Doesn't Panic -

2. It's Quick to Involve God -

3. It Rehearses the Truth -

4. It Gives Thanks -

5. It Submits to God -

6. It Persists -

Q26: Can you think of anything for which you need to "forgive God" before you will be able and willing to completely trust him?

SECTION THREE

Loving God by OBEYING Him

When I think of obedience, the first thing that comes to mind is dogs. It's what you expect from a pet or a soldier or a young child: to do what they're told. Most people wouldn't automatically associate it with love because it doesn't have a very warm tone to it.

But the Bible's connection between the two is explicit. Of all the ways it tells us to love God, obedience gets the most attention. Putting it plainly, Jesus said:

> 21a "Those who accept my commandments and obey them are the ones who love me. ...
> 24a Anyone who doesn't love me will not obey me." (John 14:21a, 24a, NLT)

> Loving God means keeping his commandments. (1 John 5:3)

It's possible to obey God and *not* love him. But it's *not* possible to love God and remain disobedient to him by ignoring or resisting what he wants. Loving God involves *more* than obeying him, but it never involves *less*.

> 22 On judgment day many will say to me (Jesus), "Lord! Lord! We prophesied in your name and cast out demons in your name and performed many miracles in your name." 23 But I will reply, "I never knew you. Get away from me, you who break God's laws." (Matthew 7:22–23)

Unfortunately, the Bible's stress on this point can spoil our motivation if we're not paying attention. We can start to think of doing the right thing as an end in itself or all that really matters, thus leaving out the *loving* part of it. Legalists do that. They're more concerned about being right, looking good, fitting in and avoiding criticism than they are about God himself.

Q1: Do you see any of that tendency in yourself?

In contrast, the kind of obedience God loves is a means to an end, a tangible way for us to express our love for him. At its core is a sincere desire to please and honor him, to make him smile, warm his heart and avoid everything that doesn't. Jesus was full of it.

> "I have come down from heaven not to do my will but to do the will of him who sent me." (John 6:38)

> "...I seek not to please myself but him who sent me." (John 5:30b)

> "My food," said Jesus, "is to do the will of him who sent me and to finish his work." (John 4:34)

That always came first. It was more important to him than eating. Everything else could wait, and nothing on earth satisfied him more.

Q2: How do you think a person becomes like that?

God's intention is to transform us into people who resemble Jesus in every way that matters. The process is referred to as "sanctification" or "becoming holy/Christlike/spiritually mature." As you would suspect, it doesn't come quickly or easily. Some of our poor attitudes and behaviors are deeply embedded, and we're also facing some stiff opposition. But God's Word reassures us that his Spirit is constantly at work to guide, steady, replenish and enable us to live as he desires.

There are numerous things we can do to cooperate with him and build-up the spiritual attitudes we need to become more dependably and lovingly obedient. Those are what we are responsible for, so let's consider six that are absolutely necessary:

1. **Rest Assured in God's Love for You**
2. **Humbly Submit to Jesus's Authority**
3. **Get Familiar with God's Will**
4. **Focus on Progress More than Perfection**
5. **Expect Some Fierce Opposition**
6. **Cooperate with the Holy Spirit**

Stop wallowing in **your** unworthiness and concentrate instead on how kind and loyal **he** is.

CHAPTER 11
REST ASSURED IN GOD'S LOVE FOR YOU

One day I asked my auto mechanic why he had left his job at the service department of a large dealership. He replied, "I didn't want to go to hell." They were crooked and expected him to play along, but he was unwilling. I appreciated that he had a genuine fear of God, but it wasn't obvious that he also *loved* him. Anxious compliance is better than nothing, but it isn't what God is really after, any more than it's what we want from our children.

> You have not received a spirit that makes you fearful slaves. Instead, you received God's Spirit when he adopted you as his own children. Now we call him, "Abba, Father." (Romans 8:15, NLT)

> 27 (Jesus said,) "My sheep listen to my voice; I know them, and they follow me. 28 I give them eternal life, and they shall never perish; no one will snatch them out of my hand. 29 My Father, who has given them to me, is greater than all; no one can snatch them out of my Father's hand. 30 I and the Father are one." (John 10:27–30)

Reassurances like those are meant to make us feel secure in God's love and provide us with solid ground to build on. For some, though, it's a battleground. They are habitually harassed by negative self-talk and a critical conscience that is rarely satisfied. They often suspect something is wrong with them or what they've done, and that God has withdrawn and will be displeased with them until they fix it.

They're like the young man struggling with addiction who confided to me that he felt completely unworthy whenever he entered a church. He couldn't pry his attention off of his failures and the disapproving scowl he imagined on God's face. No wonder he didn't attend very often and hadn't made much spiritual progress. His misery is familiar to many.

But here's the deal. Before you even started to care about God, he surveyed your entire life, thoroughly examined your heart and decided that he wanted you. There is now no way you can catch him by surprise or exhaust his patience or change his mind, even if you're awful. He already knew all about it and voluntarily did what was necessary to make you his forever.

[6] When we were utterly helpless, Christ came at just the right time and died for us sinners. [7] Now, most people would not be willing to die for an upright person, though someone might perhaps be willing to die for a person who is especially good. [8] But God showed his great love for us by sending Christ to die for us while we were still sinners. (Romans 5:6–8, NLT)

He means for us to take hold of this knowledge and run with it for the rest of our days; to stop wallowing in our unworthiness and concentrate instead on how kind and loyal *he* is. Paul voiced his intentions for us in these words:

[17b] ... (I pray that) your roots will grow down into God's love and keep you strong. [18] And may you have the power to understand, as all God's people should, how wide, how long, how high, and how deep his love is. [19] May you experience the love of Christ, though it is too great to understand fully. Then you will be made complete with all the fullness of life and power that comes from God. (Ephesians 3:17b–19, NLT)

When it finally sinks in that God's love for you is joyful and non-negotiable, that he will never love you more or less than he does right now, you will be more disposed to love him back. And your obedience can then become a more grateful expression of that love.

Q3: Is there any part of the last few paragraphs that you sometimes doubt? If so, when and why?

Q4: What can a person do to experience more of God's love when they're running low on it?

EXERCISE: Lots of things can shrink or boost our feelings about God and how we think he feels about us. Underline each of the following suggestions that you should take to heart, and "Star" the ones you feel stuck on or stumped by. Make sure to read all of the recommended verses.

1. *Ask him to make you aware of anything he's displeased or concerned about with you:* Psalm 139:23–24; Romans 14:22b

2. *Make sure you have humbly acknowledged and repented of every sin you're aware of (as in this example):* Psalm 51:1–17

3. *Make sure no one has something against you that you haven't sincerely tried to make right with them:* Matthew 5:23–26

4. *Make sure you're free of resentments:* Matthew 6:14–15; 18:23–35

5. *Make sure you're not resisting or ignoring anything you suspect he wants you to do:* Psalm 32:3–6

6. *Take your time to make a comprehensive gratitude list, then tell him what's on it:* Psalm 103:8–14; Romans 8:28–39; Hebrews 4:4–16; 12:6–11

7. *Admire, appreciate and praise him out loud, sometimes in song. He loves your voice:* Psalm 95:1–7

8. *Ask him to re-reassure you of his love and listen to songs that affirm it:* Hebrews 4:15–16

9. *Encourage and love-on a few people you care about who need it. Especially if you don't feel like it:* Hebrews 3:13

The words "but" and "Lord"
should never be used in the
same sentence.

CHAPTER 12
HUMBLY SUBMIT TO JESUS' AUTHORITY

[After washing their feet, Jesus said to his disciples,] 13 "You call me 'Teacher' and 'Lord,' and rightly so, for that is what I am. 14 Now that I, your Lord and Teacher, have washed your feet, you also should wash one another's feet. 15 I have set you an example that you should do as I have done for you. 16 Very truly I tell you, no servant is greater than his master, nor is a messenger greater than the one who sent him. 17 Now that you know these things, you will be blessed if you do them." (John 13:13–17)

"Why do you call me, 'Lord, Lord,' and do not do what I say?" (Luke 6:46)

For a person to be your "Lord" carries some life-defining implications:

- They hold a superior rank and occupy a higher position than you.

- They are in charge and have authority over you.

- They are your master or boss.

- They have the right to tell you what to do, even to make demands of you.

- You don't have the right to hold back, negotiate or refuse (unless they say so).

- They have the right to correct, discipline or punish you if you don't comply.

In Jesus's day, referring to a person as "Lord" *could* be a mere expression of respect, like calling him "Sir." But it doesn't sound like that's all Jesus had in mind for his disciples. He gave them orders and told them what to do as a master would with his servants. He still does that with us.

9 God exalted (Jesus) to the highest place and gave him the name that is above every name,
10 that at the name of Jesus every knee should bow, in heaven and on earth and under the earth,
11 and every tongue acknowledge that Jesus Christ is Lord, to the glory of God the Father. (Philippians 2:9–11)

20 (God) raised Christ from the dead and seated him at his right hand in the heavenly realms,
21 far above all rule and authority, power and dominion, and every name that is invoked, not only

in the present age but also in the one to come. [22] And God placed all things under his feet and appointed him to be head over everything…. (Ephesians 1:20–22)

God-loving obedience obliges us to acknowledge Jesus as both our Savior and our Lord, which then enables us to gladly comply with this appeal:

I urge you, brothers and sisters, in view of God's mercy, to offer your bodies as a living sacrifice, holy and pleasing to God—this is your true and proper worship. (Romans 12:1)

It may be helpful to accompany the offering of yourself with words like these:

- *"Lord, I surrender my will and life to you."*
- *"I'm all yours, body and soul. You are in charge from now on."*
- *"Your wish is my command. I will do whatever you want."*

Even though you *won't* always do what he wants, at least you'll *intend* to. And that's a great start.

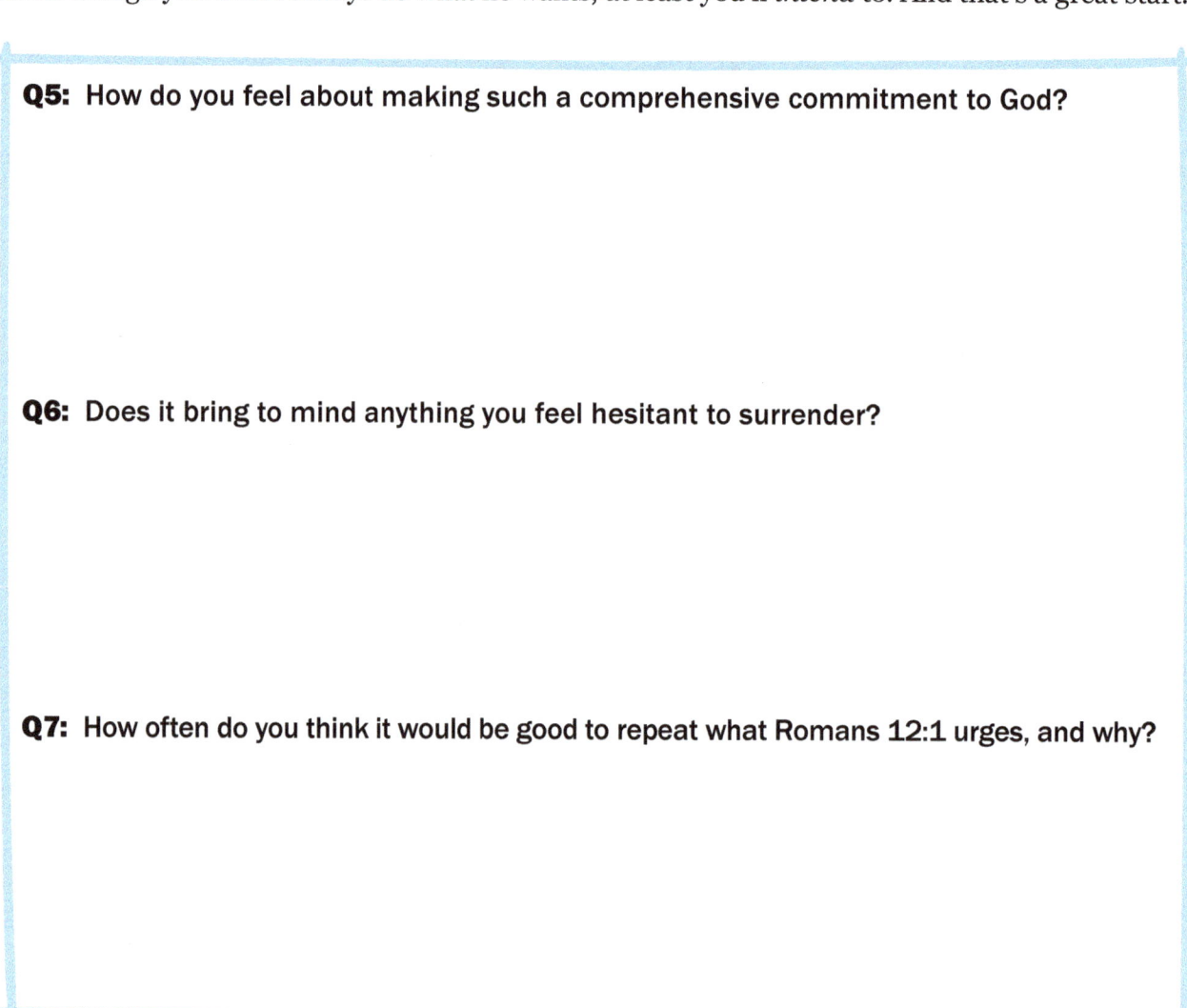

Q5: How do you feel about making such a comprehensive commitment to God?

Q6: Does it bring to mind anything you feel hesitant to surrender?

Q7: How often do you think it would be good to repeat what Romans 12:1 urges, and why?

By one Jewish way of counting, the OT contains 613 commandments. The NT contributes another thousand or so.[25] Every one of them highlights an essential facet of God's goodness, and Jesus complied with them all. Not once did he need to feel guilty for anything he did, said or even thought, because he never was guilty.

> We do not have a high priest who is unable to empathize with our weaknesses, but we have one who has been tempted in every way, just as we are—yet he did not sin. (Hebrews 4:15)

It's a huge relief to know that God understands our inability to match his Son's flawless performance. That's an expression of his **grace**. But he does want us to aim and strive for his standard as a demonstration of our devotion to him.

*The word "**grace**" refers to a free and generous gift; a charitable act; unearned acceptance; undeserved favor.*

> [14] As obedient children, do not conform to the evil desires you had when you lived in ignorance. [15] But just as he who called you is holy, so be holy in all you do; [16] for it is written: "Be holy, because I am holy." (1 Peter 1:14–16)

> [After many years of spiritual growth, Paul wrote:] [12] I don't mean to say that I have already...reached perfection. But I press on to possess that perfection for which Christ Jesus first possessed me. [13] No, dear brothers and sisters, I have not achieved it, but I focus on this one thing: Forgetting the past and looking (*reaching, stretching, straining*) forward to what lies ahead, [14] I press on to reach the end of the race and receive the heavenly prize for which God, through Christ Jesus, is calling us. ... [16] But we must hold on to the progress we have already made. (Philippians 3:12–16, NLT)

---

[25] The number is substantially lower if you combine them according to topic. The point is that there are *a lot.*

The words of Scripture are the vocabulary the Spirit most often uses to speak to us. We must become familiar with them if we hope to hear clearly from him.

CHAPTER 13
GET FAMILIAR WITH GOD'S WILL

> [15] Be very careful how you live—not as unwise but as wise, [16] making the most of every opportunity, because the days are evil. [17] Therefore do not be foolish, but understand what the Lord's will is. (Ephesians 5:15–17)

Though essential, this can get really confusing. Many think of God's will as his detailed, pre-written, minute-by-minute plan for each person's daily life that stays hidden until we discover it. It must then be followed to the letter or we risk missing-out forever on his best for us.[26] They therefore believe we must constantly search for it by listening for his voice, waiting for inner peace, looking for a sign, flipping a coin, polling our friends or "feeling led."

Q8: Which of those do you sometimes rely on to help you "hear God," and why?

Those methods *are* mentioned in the Bible and may infrequently play a role, but they also create anxiety and rob us of many daily freedoms that God means for us to enjoy. None of them are recommended as the standard way to learn his will. Instead, he wants us to think like this:

> *Your word* is a lamp for my feet, a light on my path. (Psalm 119:105)

> Direct my footsteps according to *your word*; let no sin rule over me. (Psalm 119:133)

> [9] How can a young person stay on the path of purity? By living according to *your word*. [10] I seek you with all my heart; do not let me stray from *your commands*. [11] I have hidden *your word* in my heart that I might not sin against you. (Psalm 119:9–11)

---

[26] A terrific book on this topic is *Decision Making and the Will of God*, by Gary Friesen. It carefully explains some common misunderstandings about God's will, and it provides a liberating, biblical alternative to them.

31b ... [Jesus says:] "You are truly my disciples if you remain faithful to *my teachings* (literally: 'continue in *my word*'). 32 And you will know the truth, and the truth will set you free." (John 8:31b–32, NLT)

We need to be like this guy:

97 O (Lord), how I love your instructions! I think about them all day long. 98 Your commands make me wiser than my enemies, for they are my constant guide. 99 Yes, I have more insight than my teachers, for I am always thinking of your laws. ... 103 How sweet your words taste to me; they are sweeter than honey. 104 Your commandments give me understanding; no wonder I hate every false way of life. 105 Your word is a lamp to guide my feet and a light for my path. ... 111 Your laws are my treasure; they are my heart's delight. 112 I am determined to keep your decrees to the very end. (Psalm 119:97–112, NLT)

God's priceless instructions and decrees are presented in diverse ways throughout the Bible.

One "Most Important" Commandment

This is the distillation of God's will for us into its purest and most concentrated form: "Love him first, most and fully." Get that right and you'll get everything else right in the process.[27] But it doesn't mean that God is the only one who matters.

Two Summary Commandments

Jesus isolated one of the six major ways we can express our love to God, then coupled it with The Most Important Commandment and created a matching pair. Together they express what all the other biblical commandments are promoting.

37 Love the Lord your God with all your heart and with all your soul and with all your mind. 38 This is the first and greatest commandment. 39 And the second is like it: Love your neighbor as yourself. 40 All the Law and the Prophets hang on these two commandments. (Matthew 22:37–40)

The 10 Commandments (Exodus 20:1-17)

These are all still very basic, but they provide more concrete guidance on how to obey the Two Summary Commandments. The first four describe how to love God; the remaining six expand on ways to love our neighbor.

1 God spoke all these words: 2 "I am the LORD (*Yahweh*) your God, who brought you out of...slavery.[28]

---

27 Someone paraphrased St. Augustine as saying it like this: "Love God and do whatever you please."
28 A few phrases have been edited and replaced with ellipses (...) to keep the focus on God's commandments.

³ You shall have no other gods before me.

⁴ You shall not make for yourself an image in the form of anything in heaven above or on the earth beneath or in the waters below [as an object of religious reverence]. 5 You shall not bow down to them or worship them; for I, the LORD your God, am a jealous God...

⁷ You shall not misuse (*make light of, disrespect, use flippantly or invoke to support a lie*) the name of the LORD (*Yahweh*) your God, for the LORD (*Yahweh*) will not hold anyone guiltless who misuses his name.

⁸ Remember the Sabbath day by keeping it holy. ⁹ Six days you shall labor and do all your work, ¹⁰ but the seventh day is a Sabbath to the LORD your God...

---

¹² Honor your father and your mother...

¹³ You shall not murder.

¹⁴ You shall not commit adultery.

¹⁵ You shall not steal.

¹⁶ You shall not give false testimony against your neighbor.

¹⁷ You shall not covet (*desire, lust for*) your neighbor's house or wife ... or anything that belongs to your neighbor...." (Exodus 20:1–17)

The 39 Books of the Old Testament

Some of it is peculiar and much is magnificent. Every bit is God's Word and has something valuable to teach us. But it also begs this question: "Are we, nowadays, still expected to obey *everything* it commands?" Jesus clarified:

¹⁷ Don't misunderstand why I have come. I did not come to abolish the law of Moses or the writings of the prophets. No, I came to accomplish their purpose. ¹⁸ I tell you the truth, until heaven and earth disappear, not even the smallest detail of God's law will disappear until its purpose is achieved. (Matthew 5:17–18, NLT)

The Old Covenant ceremonial, sacrificial, purification and dietary laws told God's people in fine detail how to be cleansed and worship him acceptably. But once Jesus introduced the New Covenant through his death and resurrection, those old laws became unnecessary. He completed what they set out to do; he fulfilled what they anticipated and previewed. Now it's our *faith in him* that makes us clean and fit to worship.

But there's a lot more to the pre-Jesus Bible than those outdated laws. It is packed with timeless guidance and instructions, warnings and wisdom, prohibitions and demands, examples and illustrations. It's not always easy to understand how (or if) it applies, but it's far from obsolete.

The word of our God endures forever. (Isaiah 40:8b)

¹⁶ All Scripture is God-breathed and is useful for teaching, rebuking, correcting and training in righteousness, ¹⁷ so that the servant of God may be thoroughly equipped for every good work. (2 Timothy 3:16–17)

The 27 Books of the New Testament

¹ Jesus took with him Peter, James and John the brother of James, and led them up a high mountain by themselves. ² There he was transfigured before them. his face shone like the sun, and his clothes became as white as the light. ³ Just then there appeared before them Moses and Elijah (- *key spokesmen of the OT law and prophets*), talking with Jesus. ⁴ Peter said to Jesus, "Lord, it is good for us to be here. If you wish, I will put up three shelters—one for you, one for Moses and one for Elijah." ⁵ While he was still speaking, a bright cloud covered them, and a voice from the cloud said, "This is my Son, whom I love; with him I am well pleased. Listen to *him*!" (Matthew 17:1–5)

¹⁶ Jesus: "My teaching is not my own. It comes from the one who sent me. ¹⁷ Anyone who chooses to do the will of God will find out whether my teaching comes from God or whether I speak on my own." (John 7:16–17)

²¹ (To his disciples after his resurrection, Jesus said,) "Peace be with you! As the Father has sent me, I am sending you." ²² And with that he breathed on them and said, "Receive the Holy Spirit." (John 20:21–22)

¹⁹ We (Christians) are members of (God's) household, ²⁰ built on the foundation of the apostles and prophets, with Christ Jesus himself as the chief cornerstone. (Ephesians 2:19b–20)

Jesus is the one through whom God has chosen to explain himself and his will to the human race for the rest of time. He and his original emissaries are the teachers we're to consult when we wonder how to interpret/apply the OT or what God wants from us in a particular situation.[29]

So the main way we come to know the will of God is through the Word of God as his Spirit makes it alive and relevant to us. Every day we're conscious it beckons us to enjoy private sessions with him, during which he is pleased to explain as much about himself and his ways as we care to know, ...*so that* we can grow to love him more as he deserves.

¹² The word of God is alive and active. Sharper than any double-edged sword, it penetrates even to dividing soul and spirit, joints and marrow; it judges the thoughts and attitudes of the heart. ¹³ Nothing in all creation is hidden from God's sight. Everything is uncovered and laid bare before the eyes of him to whom we must give account. (Hebrew 4:12–13)

---

[29] Those people in the world who don't (yet) know about Jesus have a spiritual predicament that only God can remedy. How He intends to deal with them is at least partially explained in Romans 1:18-20 and 2:9-16.

EXERCISE: Read the following three passages in your Bible to better acquaint yourself with the sort of good person God wants you to be. These are the primary type of things his will consists of. As you read them, understand that writing in your Bible doesn't defile, but *personalizes* it. So:

1. Underline the parts you're (pretty much) in compliance with.

2. Put a question mark next to those you're unsure of.

3. Circle the parts you're not consistently living up to at this time.

    ◦ Matthew 5–7 (all three chapters)

    ◦ Galatians 5:19–23

    ◦ Ephesians 4:17–5:21

Q8: Based on all you just read, in what few ways do you believe your character, lifestyle and efforts to obey the Lord are more pleasing to him now than they used to be?

Q9: What few things does God especially want you to stop, do or change? Be specific. After you write them down, number-prioritize them according to their importance, talk to God about them and set a date by when you will mention them to someone you trust.

Interacting with God's Word in these ways trains your conscience to speak to you more quickly and accurately, with his voice instead of only your own (or someone else's). As you've just seen, his Spirit will use it to reveal that you're doing really well in some areas and not so well in others. That's why you will also need to learn how to do what the next chapter urges.

"I freely admit: I haven't yet attained to all that God intends for me. I'm not complete. But this one thing I do: forgetting what's behind and straining forward to what's ahead, I press on...."
(Paul in Philippians 3:13-14a, Paraphrase)

CHAPTER 14
FOCUS ON PROGRESS MORE THAN PERFECTION

You may have heard that all sins are alike, but it's not true.[30] Some we can crush like a spider with a swift smack. But others quickly jump and skitter away when we try to kill them. Why that's so is important to understand.

Some Sins Can be Handled Decisively

[29] (Jesus said,) "If your right eye causes you to stumble, gouge it out and throw it away. It is better for you to lose one part of your body than for your whole body to be thrown into hell. [30] And if your right hand causes you to stumble, cut it off and throw it away. It is better for you to lose one part of your body than for your whole body to go into hell." (Matthew 5:29–30)

In other words, sometimes you can just stop what you've been doing wrong. Be done with it. Get rid of it and everything that feeds it.[31] Be abrupt and harsh if you must. If it tries to "grow back" later on, repeat the process until it finally dies down and out. Some fish you catch won't stop flopping until you knock them in the head. If you later slip-up or relapse in a bigger way, promptly talk to God and someone else about why it keeps happening and how to respond better next time.

Some Sins Are in a Different League

You can try to "put them to death" or "cast them out" or "let them go" all at once, but they seem to be holding on to you more than you are to them, like a python coiled in a death grip around your neck.

When I became a Christian, the Spirit quickly led me to eliminate some of my more obvious shortcomings. Almost immediately I stopped stealing, using illicit drugs, lying and looking at

---

[30] Unless what one means is that even "small" sins matter and should be addressed. Of course that's so. But some sins are far more serious and consequential than others! See 1 Corinthians 6:18 and Jude 22.

[31] Certain songs, movies, shows, websites, games, people, associations and activities expose us to evil, give it access to our hearts and awaken it within us. Some of them are very difficult to unsee, unhear or unfeel. Some take on a life of their own and become addictive. For love's sake we need to be conscientious about pre-screening, editing or just plain eliminating them. Numerous resources are available to help if you do a little research.

porn. It was harder to stop swearing, but after a short while it seemed that I was mostly sin-free most of the time.

Then I got married and rapidly discovered that I was a self-absorbed, emotionally fragile, needy, compulsive, demanding, spiritually shallow person prone to ugly outbursts of anger. And I couldn't change those things simply by deciding to or praying, even with fasting.

Over time, one thing I learned about obstinate, recurring sins is that they are *more* than just bad attitudes or disobedient behaviors. They are also determined efforts to get something we want or to shield us from something we dislike, as in these examples:

> When Eve saw that the [forbidden] fruit of the tree was good for food and pleasing to the eye, and also desirable for gaining wisdom, she took some and ate it. She also gave some to her husband, who was with her, and he ate it. (Genesis 3:6)

Once arrested, Jesus was bound and taken to be questioned by the high priest. Peter followed at a distance and joined some bystanders warming themselves by a fire in the dim courtyard. After a little while, they said to him:

> [73] ... "Surely you are one of (Jesus's followers); your accent gives you away." [74] Then he began to call down curses, and he swore to them, "I don't know the man!'" (Matthew 26:73b–74)

> [14] A person gets tempted when they are enticed and ensnared by their own evil desire. Then, after their desire has conceived into a decision, it gives birth to sin... (James 1:14–15a, Paraphrase)

A desire is evil and its actions sinful if our good Father forbids it for some reason. He doesn't want us to have it, at least not at the time or in the way we want it. What gets us into trouble is our unwillingness to submit to his authority or accept his prohibition, because the thing we desire is too *important* to us.[32] We may even believe that we *must* have it. We *need* it because we'll be miserable or lost without it.

Why would we believe such things? Perhaps it's because our souls continue to feel leftover pain, emptiness, shame, sadness, insecurity, loneliness, resentment or fear from injuries and wounds we suffered many years prior. That has been true for me, and some of them are still not fully mended.

That's one reason why some sins are so insanely difficult to resist and require more than a simple decision to squash. We can overcome them only by degrees and with help. We need supernatural insight to answer questions like these:

1. *Why are my reactions so intense at times?*

2. *Why am I so impacted by how others treat me?*

3. *Why do I need life to go a certain way?*

---

[32] Like Gollum's "Precious" in *The Lord of the Rings* by J.R.R. Tolkien.

4. *What am I so afraid of?*

5. *What do I believe I can't do without?*

6. *How can I need it **less** or do without it **entirely**?*

7. *How can I more consistently get what I need from God in ways that he approves?*

> "We must worship Christ with the help of the Holy Spirit, adoring him until our hearts find him more beautiful than the object we thought we had to have" [33]
>
> – Timothy Keller

Learning these things typically involves a bruising, long-term struggle with ups and downs that resemble a fluctuating stock market graph. We therefore need to focus more on *progress* than *perfection*. A good motto for us could be, "Please Be Patient; God Is Not Finished With Me Yet."

He who began a good work in you will carry it on to completion until the day of Christ Jesus *(when he returns)*. (Philippians 1:6b)

When Christ appears, we shall be like him, for we shall see him as he is. (1 John 3:2b)

[On that day God will] present you before his glorious presence without fault and with great joy. (Jude 24b)

Q10: Which of your feelings and reactions sometimes seem bigger or more negative than is warranted by the current circumstances?

Q11: What do you think makes them so?

---

[33] Timothy Keller, *Galatians For You*, [Charlotte: The Good Book Company, 2012], 157). Passages like these can help us to do so: James 4:7–10; Psalm 73:25–28; Isaiah 55:1–2; Philippians 4:10–13.

Q12: What temptations or ungodly impulses do you sometimes experience as too difficult to resist, and what do you think makes them so?

What They Are	What Makes Them So DIFFICULT

Q13: Does anything mentioned in your last few answers seem to be linked to negative experiences in your past? Explain.

Q14: How can people become more free from (= less influenced by) the hangover effects of negative experiences in their past? Write your answer(s) first, then read the passage below and see if it adds anything to your thoughts.

7b I [Paul] was given a thorn in my flesh, a messenger from Satan to torment me and keep me from becoming proud. 8 Three different times I begged the Lord to take it away. 9 Each time he said, "My grace is all you need. My power works best in weakness." So now I am glad to boast about my weaknesses, so that the power of Christ can work through me. 10 That's why I take pleasure in my weaknesses, and in the insults, hardships, persecutions, and troubles that I suffer for Christ. For when I am weak, then I am strong. (2 Corinthians 12:7b-10, NLT)

While answering the last five questions, you may have detected an undesirable but influential link between your past and present. If so, it could be liberating for you to talk with someone who is qualified to help you understand and "disconnect" it. Our spiritual, emotional, psychological and physical health are complexly intertwined and interdependent. Unresolved problems in one area can seriously impact the others, and sometimes we need skillful help to untangle them.

CHAPTER 15
EXPECT SOME FIERCE OPPOSITION

Nobody likes to be told what to believe or how to behave. So we need to remind ourselves that God doesn't make rules, say "no" or set boundaries just to assert his superiority and boss us around.

- He *sees* every detail of what's going on and what's going to happen.
- He *always* wants and works to secure what's good for those he loves.
- We can *always* assume that his commandments are for our good.

Even so, what are the chances that we're always going to do what he tells us? ZERO! And why is that? What's wrong with us? Why aren't our faith and determination enough to make us reliably obedient? Why do we so often find ourselves feeling, thinking about, being attracted to and saying/doing things we know are bad? Is the problem *inside* or *outside* of us?

The right answer is *Yes!* The Bible identifies three hellish adversaries that incessantly oppose and resist our best intentions. The first two are external to us; the third is an inherited flaw in our humanity.

1. The Devil

Like God, he is a spirit: a conscious personality without a body. Unlike God, he is limited in every way as all creatures are. He apparently began life as one of the many beautiful and powerful angels God created before humans. But at some point he grew discontent, refused to accept the boundaries God set for him, went renegade and became feral.[34] The name "Satan" defines him as an enemy and an adversary; calling him a "devil" refers to his pathetic penchant for slandering, criticizing and smearing others.

We know fairly little about him, but the Bible's descriptions are uniformly repulsive. Imagine the worst atrocities that sick and evil people commit and you'll have a glimpse of what he's capable of. He is a megalomaniac tyrant who believes he is worthy of adoration; a psychopathic, malevolent, deceitful, cold, cruel and rebellious outcast who loves to masquerade as an angel of light.[35]

---

[34] He also influenced many other angels to follow his lead. See Matthew 25:41 and Revelation 12:7-9.
[35] 2 Corinthians 11:14.

He was a murderer from the beginning, not holding to the truth, for there is no truth in him. When he lies, he speaks his native language, for he is a liar and the father of lies. (John 8:44b)

... That ancient serpent called the devil, or Satan, ...leads the whole world astray. (Revelation 12:9)

He has accomplished that appalling result primarily by getting people to accept and act upon the thoughts he plants in their minds, either directly or through others. So defending ourselves against him will require us to intercept and counter the ones he's trying to use on us.

EXERCISE: Read through the following list of examples in the left column and underline any that "sound familiar" to you. Adjust or rewrite them to better resemble what you actually think, and add a couple of your own on the blank lines. After you've read the final line in the left column, answer **Q15** (just below it) to fill-in the right column with some crisp "Counter Thoughts."

DEVILISH THOUGHTS	COUNTER-THOUGHTS
Thoughts that Entice Me to Sin	**Thoughts that Can Protect Me from Sin**
I don't have to put up with this. I deserve better.	
Life has been really stressful. I've been under a lot of pressure and worked hard. I earned this.	
I deserve to relax and have some fun.	
I need this. It's too good to pass up; it'll be amazing/feel great.	
I'm not hurting anyone. It won't matter that much. It's not a big deal.	
Nothing terrible is going to happen. Others do worse things and get away with it.	
I may never have an opportunity like this again.	
I can handle it. A little bit won't hurt. I can stop whenever I want.	
Nobody's perfect. God doesn't expect me to be.	
What good does it do to be good all the time?	
God understands and will forgive me. I can start over with him any time.	
No one will know or needs to know.	
There's no going back now.	

DEVILISH THOUGHTS	COUNTER-THOUGHTS
Thoughts that Discourage and Weaken Me	**Thoughts to Encourage and Strengthen Me**
The fact that I keep sinning in the same way(s) proves I'm not a true Christian.	
There is no way God will forgive me for that.	
This is a complete disaster.	
Things are never going to change or get better.	
There is no hope.	
Things will never be as good again.	
It's just not worth trying any more.	
My motives are always mixed / bad / selfish, so what I do isn't good / worthy.	
I'm a failure / a fake / a hypocrite / a _____ .	
I'm no good. I only cause problems / trouble.	
People would be better off without me.	
God has distanced himself and is punishing me because of my sin.	
I'm not important. I don't matter.	
Nobody really cares. I'm not wanted. I'm alone.	
Someone is always unhappy with me.	
Nothing I do matters or works.	
What's the point of continuing / trying?	
I've really blown it now. The damage is done; everything that matters is ruined / lost.	

Q15: How do you suppose the Lord wants you to respond to each of the thoughts you underlined? Write your "counters" and "rebuttals" next to them in the right column, above.

> **Q16:** Can you detect anything else in your life or relationships that the devil is trying to influence? If so, what are you doing/going to do about it?

We needn't fear or obsess over the devil, because "the Spirit who lives in (us) is greater than the spirit who lives in the world" (1 John 4:4b). But we mustn't ignore what he's up to. Until the day we celebrate God casting him forever into the lake of fire (Revelation 20:10), we need to...

> [8] Be alert and of sober mind. Your enemy the devil prowls around like a roaring lion looking for someone to devour. [9] Resist him, standing firm in the faith, because you know that the family of believers throughout the world is undergoing the same kind of sufferings. (1 Peter 5:8–9)

> [9] This, then, is how you should pray: ... [13] "Lead us not into temptation, but deliver us from the evil one." (Matthew 6:9, 13)[36]

> [10] Finally, be strong in the Lord and in his mighty power. [11] Put on the full armor of God, so that you can take your stand against the devil's schemes. (Ephesians 6:10–11)[37]

Another enemy of our faith and love for God is...

2. The World

This isn't referring to "mother nature" or the planet we inhabit, but to all of the anti-God contaminants and influences in the world around us that the devil uses to lure people away from God and his ways.

> *The book of Revelation likens them to the ancient city of **Babylon**, a symbol of all that is arrogant, opulent, self-indulgent, corrupt, violent, oppressive, idolatrous, immoral and destined for God's judgment.*

> We know that we are children of God, and the whole world is under the control of the evil one. (1 John 5:19)

---

[36] This prayer addresses our frequent need for God to prevent the devil from inserting thoughts into our minds, or at least to make us more aware of when he does, so that we can quickly deal with them.

[37] These two verses introduce an extended, detailed passage on how to resist the devil that deserves much more attention than we can give it here. See *all* of Ephesians 6:10-18.

15 Therefore do not love this world, filled as it is with so many ideas, beliefs, values, desires, attitudes, options and ways of behaving that God disapproves. People who love those things show that they don't really love the Father. 16 For three of this world's worst features—the craving of the flesh, the craving of the eyes and self-congratulating pride—do not come from the Father but are part of the evil in this world. (1 John 2:15–16, Paraphrase)

Satan has concealed countless snares and anti-personnel mines along the roads we all travel. So we must stay tuned to the Spirit's warnings and vigilantly guard against "worldly" involvements that could do us harm or compromise the purity of our devotion to Jesus. Sometimes it will be enough for us simply to exercise caution and moderation, but we will also need to entirely avoid and reject some things, even though they *are* enjoyable.

> **Q17:** What are some "worldly" things (ideas, beliefs, values, desires, enjoyments, attitudes or activities) that you need to manage more carefully or shun more completely because they have a spiritually distracting or compromising effect on you?

The third adversary we have to grapple with is the most incessant and treacherous:

3. The Flesh

14 We know that (God's) law is spiritual; but I am unspiritual, sold as a slave to sin. 15 I do not understand what I do. For what I want to do I do not do, but what I hate I do. 16 And if I do what I do not want to do, I agree that the law is good. 17 As it is, it is no longer I myself who do it, but it is sin living in me. 18 For I know that good itself does not dwell in me, that is, in my sinful nature ('flesh"). For I have the desire to do what is good, but I cannot carry it out. 19 For I do not do the good I want to do, but the evil I do not want to do—this I keep on doing. 20 Now if I do what I do not want to do, it is no longer I who do it, but it is sin living in me that does it. 21 So I find this law at work: Although I want to do good, evil is right there with me. 22 For in my inner being I delight in God's law; 23 but I see another law at work in me, waging war against the law of my mind and making me a prisoner of the law of sin at work within me. 24 What a wretched man I am! Who will rescue me from this body that is subject to death? (Romans 7:14–24)

The label Paul used for his root problem with disobedience was "sin living within" him. It is also ours. We typically think of "sin" as something we do wrong, an offense against God. But Paul was talking about something less tangible. Some call it the "sinful nature." He referred to it as his "flesh," but it isn't merely the physical body.

*It's useful to call it "capital-s **S**in" and define it as an internal energy that disposes us to commit "small-s sin**s**."*

Picture it as a decaying tank of sewage sunken deep within us, endlessly leaking impure images, thoughts, words, feelings, attitudes and desires into us, encouraging us to approve of what the devil and the world offer, urging us to assert ourselves and disregard God.

Q18: What kinds of things do you regularly experience that are probably caused by your "flesh?"

CONCLUSION: Every day of this life we have to re-brace ourselves to push back against anti-God influences and pressures directed at us by the World, the Devil, and our Flesh. They can be formidable and make it extremely challenging to live a life of consistent obedience to God. No wonder there are so few of us who closely resemble Jesus in our morals, attitudes, choices and treatment of others. It's understandable.

But it isn't okay and it's not inevitable. We need to bring something more effective than our fists to this gun fight. The final chapter of this section explains the powerful resource God has provided so we can do just that.

CHAPTER 16

COOPERATE WITH THE HOLY SPIRIT

He is God's Answer to Our Dilemma

Alcoholics Anonymous published its *Big Book* in 1939 to help people live sober. Part of what made it so successful was the simple wisdom of statements like,

> *"Lack of power, that was our dilemma. We had to find a power by which we could live, and it had to be a Power greater than ourselves."*[37]

That dilemma has been universally true for all time! But a prophet of God proposed its solution long before Bill W. showed up, some 600 years before Christ.

> 26 "I will give you a new heart and put a new spirit in you; I will remove from you your heart of stone and give you a heart of flesh. 27 And I will put my Spirit in you and move you to follow my decrees and be careful to keep my laws." (Ezekiel 36:26–27)

At the last supper when Jesus announced his upcoming departure, it didn't sit well with the Twelve. The idea was unimaginable to them after three-plus years together. He was their spiritual lifeline, and they thought he was going to include them in his glorious plan to rule the world as God's King! This is how he responded to their misguided expectations and sinking hearts:

> 16 "I will ask the Father, and he will give you another Advocate *(Helper, Counselor)* who will never leave you. 17 He is the Holy Spirit, who leads into all truth. The world cannot receive him, because it isn't looking for him and doesn't recognize him. But you know him, because he lives with you now and later will be in you. 18 No, I will not abandon you as orphans—I will come to you. (John 14:16–18) ... 7 Very truly I tell you, it is for your good that I am going away. Unless I go away, the Advocate will not come to you; but if I go, I will send him to you." (John 16:7)

---

37 *Big Book of Alcoholics Anonymous*, p. 45.

If we combine the highlights of those verses with later references to the Holy Spirit,[38] it's obvious why Jesus thought leaving was such a great idea. Here's an amplified paraphrase of what he was saying:

> "I'm not leaving you behind entirely, just changing how I'll be with you. I'm going to relocate myself from being temporarily *alongside* you where I have only limited access, to living permanently *inside* you where I will have full access to all that you are. I will do that by means of the Holy Spirit, who is every bit as much "God" as I and the Father are. Since he is the Spirit of God and also *my* Spirit, the Spirit of Christ, I myself will be in you as him."

Those arrangements apply as much to us now as they did to Jesus's original audience. Six weeks later Peter made this declaration to a crowd of thousands gathered from around the world:

> [38] Each of you must repent of your sins and turn to God, and be baptized in the name of Jesus Christ for the forgiveness of your sins. Then you will receive the gift of the Holy Spirit. [39] This promise is to you, to your children, and to those far away—all who have been called by the Lord our God. (Acts 2:38–39)

Every person who calls on Jesus to be their Savior and Lord instantly becomes his new home and earthly temple. But just because he lives in us doesn't mean he's completely or automatically in charge of us right from the start.

> *For one thing, he doesn't entirely shield us from the devil or the world outside of us, nor does he eliminate the influence of "Sin" inside of us. Not yet.*

Until we see Jesus's face and our transformation is completed, each of us will be a walking civil war, a battle with ourselves in which *both* sides experience victories and setbacks.

> The sinful nature (*"flesh"/Sin within us*) wants to do evil, which is just the opposite of what the Spirit wants. And the Spirit gives us desires that are the opposite of what the sinful nature desires. These two forces are constantly fighting each other, so you are not free to carry out your good intentions. (Galatians 5:17, NLT)

That description doesn't sound especially hopeful, but it isn't God's final word on the subject. We aren't yet able to live as God intends in every situation, but he doesn't leave us lying naked and helpless on the arena floor, destined only for humiliation and defeat. On the contrary, we can confidently expect his Spirit to provide us with the essential resources we need to become increasingly consistent. For example:

---

[38] Like Romans 8:9b–11a ... You are controlled by **the Spirit** if you have **the Spirit of God** living in you. (And remember that those who do not have **the Spirit of Christ** living in them do not belong to him at all.) [10] And **Christ** lives within you, so even though your body will die because of sin, **the Spirit** gives you life because you have been made right with God. [11a] **The Spirit of God**, who raised Jesus from the dead, lives in you.... (*Notice that he is identified in four distinct, but overlapping ways in those three brief verses.*)

1. He will internally prompt and guide us to recognize temptations and discern God's will.

> All who are led by the Spirit of God are the children of God. (Romans 8:14)

> So I say, walk by *(heed the instructions of)* the Spirit and you will not gratify the desires of the flesh. (Galatians 5:16)

2. He will continually renew within us an intensified *determination* to do God's will and a fortified *ability* to actually do it.

> God is working in you, giving you the desire and the power to do what pleases him. (Philippians 2:13, NLT)

> (God:) "I will put my Spirit in you and move you to follow my decrees and be careful to keep my laws." (Ezekiel 36:27)

3. He will regularly pray on our behalf because he knows exactly what we need but don't know how to ask.

> [26] The Holy Spirit helps us in our weakness. For example, we don't know what God wants us to pray for. But the Holy Spirit prays for us with groanings that cannot be expressed in words. [27] And the Father who knows all hearts knows what the Spirit is saying, for the Spirit pleads for us believers in harmony with God's own will. (Romans 8:26–27, NLT)

So even when you feel the opposite of stable and confident, the God's-honest truth about you is this:

> Dear children, you are from God and are able to overcome your spiritual enemies, because the one who is in you is greater than the evil that opposes you in this world. (1 John 4:4, Paraphrase)

> You [therefore] have no obligation to do what your sinful nature urges you to do. (Romans 8:12, NLT)

We are no longer spiritually powerless to resist and overcome evil. Consistent obedience is *possible*. We just need to *cooperate* with the Spirit and *utilize* what he provides in order to achieve it. How to do that is what the rest of this section is about.

Q19: Which of the last few ideas do you find the most encouraging, and why?

Enlist the Holy Spirit's Aid

If by the Spirit you put to death the misdeeds of the body, you will live. (Romans 8:13b)

That single verse suggests several key ideas:

- "Capital-s Sin" within us desires to express itself through the members of our bodies.

- It's up to *us* to prevent that from happening; *we* are responsible to "put it to death." More is required of us than "letting go and letting God." Willpower and effort are necessary.

- But succeeding at this isn't entirely up to us. The way Christians can finally overcome sin is "by means of" or "through the agency of" the Holy Spirit. It is ultimately *his* determination and power that makes our obedience possible.

Okay, great! But what does that mean we're actually supposed to do? What is the difference between our role and the Spirit's role? Surprisingly, Paul doesn't say much, and the rest of Scripture provides less detail on this topic than you might expect. Apparently, the Spirit intends each of us to develop and personalize our own ways of interacting and relying on him.

I've discovered that I must frequently replenish my leaking soul through extended, undistracted times of seeking, unburdening, learning from, delighting in, submitting to and reaffirming my confidence in the One who loves me. Neglecting these things for even a few days leaves me feeling dry, dull, listless and irritable.

I have also found it helpful to break Paul's general instruction (*to "put to death the body's misdeeds by means of the Spirit"*) into more definite actions. These steps were frustratingly hard at first because my counter-impulses are so strong, but they have grown easier and more automatic with practice.[39] In an effort to make them memorable I've chosen an "R" word to represent each one.

Whenever we're about to enter (or are already involved in) a situation/interaction where we might respond poorly or ineffectively, this is one way to consciously enlist and draw upon the Spirit's aid:

1. **RESTRAIN** your initial impulse to proceed or speak or act. It may be extremely difficult to do, but rarely will your first reaction be the best one. People who prefer to shoot from the hip must often reload with regret.

2. **RECALL** that the Holy Spirit is right there to guide and strengthen you from within to handle the situation as God desires.

3. **REQUEST** what you need from the Holy Spirit and expect him to respond, even if it isn't immediately or exactly as you want. Remember, he's less interested in changing your experience than your perspective and your attitude.

4. **RESPOND** as God desires, as best you can.

5. **REVIEW** with the Lord how you handled the situation, and try to learn something from it for next time.

---

[39] If you distrust step-by-step solutions (or just dislike the letter "R"), by all means devise something that works better for you.

How A Real-life Scenario Might Play Out

You're conversing with someone who is starting to get heated or becoming disrespectful. You're tightening up inside and thinking of words that would feel great to say but aren't helpful. So...

1. **RESTRAIN** – Don't comment or make a face or walk away. Just hold on for a moment.

2. **RECALL** – Shift your attention onto the Lord who is present and ready to handle the situation *with* you. (Time needed: three seconds.) If necessary and possible, you can politely withdraw to pray and collect your thoughts. (Time needed: at least a few minutes.)

3. **REQUEST** – the Spirit to give you more of his compassion to care for this person, his help to control your tongue, and clarity regarding how he wants you to respond. Thank him for the help he's going to provide, even if you don't feel it, and determine to do whatever he wants you to. (Time needed: 10 seconds.)

   If you have a bit longer, you can also ask him for wisdom to understand the situation as he does, why you're feeling upset, how you might be contributing to the problem and what, specifically, he wants you to say/do next. Then pause to "listen" for his response and strategize your next move. (Time needed: at least a few minutes.)

4. **RESPOND** – Re-enter the situation and do your best to follow the Spirit's lead. If you simply cannot, take an extended break until you're clearer and more composed, then try.

5. **REVIEW** – Ask the Lord (and perhaps another witness) to clarify what happened and how well you handled it so you can grow in your ability to cooperate with ("walk by") the Spirit.

Q20: In what circumstances might you need to implement an approach like this, and how would you go about it?

As you think through possible scenarios like those, you'll see how crucial it is to stay in the closest-possible contact with the Spirit so you can clearly hear his voice and sense his guidance. There are numerous other things we can make use of to help us with this. They are sometimes referred to as "means of grace"—things that enhance and refresh our experience of God. Let's group them all under the heading of ways to...

Stay Filled with the Holy Spirit

An old fable tells of two wolves living inside every person that are unable to peacefully coexist and often fight each other for dominance. The one that wins is the one you feed.

One of the *Bible's* ways to apply that lesson is by telling us:

> Don't get drunk with wine, because that leads to wastefulness and reckless abandon. Instead, stay filled with the Holy Spirit. (Ephesians 5:18, Paraphrase)

Commanding us to "stay filled with the Holy Spirit" is NOT just another way of telling us to "*Be obedient,*" as though the verse simply said, "*Let the Holy Spirit control you by doing whatever he says.*"

*It's actually telling us how to make it **easier** for the Holy Spirit to influence our behavior by first making us more alert, accessible and responsive to him.*

The analogy of intoxication is helpful. Getting drunk is a two-step sequence of cause and effect. The more you imbibe, the more influential the alcohol becomes until you are "under its control" or "filled" with it, which then governs your behavior. The difference between the Spirit and alcohol is that we never need to get more of him into us, because he is always *entirely* present. We can, though, become more filled with him in a different sense.

Imagine you're falling in love with someone and want to grow even closer. How would you go about making them a larger and more enthralling presence in your heart? You would reflect often on what you cherish about them and how they make you feel. You would call, text, meet whenever possible, do activities together, ask questions, be attentive, share deeply, care about what they care about, express affection, avoid what might offend or hurt them, apologize quickly if you do, and so on.

Similarly there are a variety of things we can do to "amplify" and stay captivated by (filled with) the Spirit's presence within us.[40] These make it more natural for us to sense his love and reassurance, experience his peace, recognize his voice, understand his point of view, discern his

---

[40] In Ephesians 5:19-21, the first five recommendations (in **bold** text, below) are written in Greek as participles. That verb form is often used to indicate the ***means*** by which we can do what we're told. If that's the case here, they are telling us ***how*** to stay filled with the Spirit (and not just what *results* from doing so, as many teach). That interpretation makes perfect sense in this context where Paul has just told us what to do—*stay filled with the Spirit*—and then explains several ***ways*** to do so successfully.

guidance, feel what he feels and want what he wants—all of which support and energize our basic commitment to love God through our obedience. Here are several of the tools he urges us to use so we can enjoy those benefits more often and more intensely:

1. Music

Feeding Christian songs into your heart can be such a powerful mood modifier and perspective shifter! Sing them enthusiastically to God when you're at church and play them in the background during your daily routines. Plant their melodies and words in you where they can spread their scent into your soul and help to make the Spirit's presence more evident there.

> **Speaking** to one another with psalms, hymns, and spiritual songs, singing and making music from your heart to the Lord.... (Ephesians 5:19)

2. Thanksgiving

Throughout each day, acknowledge God as responsible for everything good that happens, including the things that don't initially appear to be good. Revoke the permission you give yourself to voice all your negative, irritable or critical reactions, and quickly apologize when they slip out. They grieve the Holy Spirit and easily become habitual if you don't. Determine instead to trust God and practice gratitude by...

> ... always **giving thanks** to God the Father for everything, in the name of our Lord Jesus Christ.... (Ephesians 5:20)

3. Serving

Jesus summarized his approach to life by saying, "I am among you as someone who serves" (Luke 22:27b). He moved through every day noticing, stopping and giving his full attention to people as though they were *truly* important to him. He viewed himself as here for them. **They weren't distractions from his work. They *were* his work.**

That's how Paul was thinking when he added this next way to stay filled with the Spirit, then spent the following six paragraphs in Ephesians elaborating on how to do it.

> **Submitting** to one another out of reverence for Christ. (Ephesians 5:21)

God designed us to need rest and time for ourselves. That's a given. But sometimes when you're feeling depleted or moody or "off," the quickest way to refill your heart is by blessing someone else. The people who need you are pretty easy to spot if you'll just pray and look for them.

> 3 ... Be humble, thinking of others as better (*more important*) than yourselves. 4 Don't look out only for your own interests, but take an interest in others, too. (Philippians 2:3b–4, NLT)

Give, and it will be given to you. A good measure, pressed down, shaken together and running over, will be poured into your lap. For with the measure you use, it will be measured to you. (Luke 6:38)

You will be enriched in every way so that you can be generous on every occasion. (2 Corinthians 9:11)

4. Scripture

Along with prayer, there is no more direct way to nurture closeness with God's Spirit than to cultivate your love for his Word.

> [1] Oh, the joys of those who ... [2] delight in the law of the LORD, meditating on it day and night. [3] They are like trees planted along the riverbank, bearing fruit each season. Their leaves never wither, and they prosper in all they do. (Psalm 1:1a–3, NLT)

Once we started following Jesus we were immediately enrolled into a lifelong apprenticeship as his disciples/students. Since then our abiding assignment has been to spend enough time with our Teacher to absorb every word he says *so that* we can live accordingly.

> The student is not above the teacher, but everyone who is fully trained will be like their teacher. (Luke 6:40)

> Do your best (*be diligent, work hard*) to present yourself to God as one approved, a worker who does not need to be ashamed and who correctly handles the word of truth. (2 Timothy 2:15)

> [31] To (those) who had believed him, Jesus said, "If you hold to (*remain, stay, continue in*) my teaching, you are really my disciples. [32] Then you will know the truth, and the truth will set you free." (John 8:31–32)

5. Prayer (of many kinds including confession, worship, appreciation, requests, pleas, etc.)

It's totally normal for our sense of God's presence to fade and to feel less connected to him at times. But many kinds of prayer enable us to re-encounter him in ways that re-illuminate our heart with his radiance. Sometimes we just need to stay at it for a while without interruption, like warming ourselves by a fire.

> As we gaze upon the Lord's glory and engage him with open hearts, we will be transformed by his Spirit into his image from one degree of glory to the next. (2 Corinthians 4:18, Paraphrase)

> [8] I keep my eyes always on the LORD. With him at my right hand, I will not be shaken. [9] Therefore my heart is glad and my tongue rejoices.... [11] You make known to me the path of life; you will fill me with joy in your presence, with eternal pleasures at your right hand. (Psalm 16:8–11)

6. Fellowship

Early Christians called this "koinonia": sharing their lives and faith with each other in deeply personal ways that bonded them as a family and enriched everyone's experience of God. It even worked for introverts! It's not always easy to find nowadays, so you may need to initiate it by gathering a few people who love God and want to grow together by using some variation of this first century example:

> 43 They devoted themselves to the apostles' teaching and to fellowship, to the breaking of bread and to prayer. ... 44 All the believers were together and had everything in common. 45 They sold property and possessions to give to anyone who had need. 46 Every day they continued to meet together in the temple courts. They broke bread in their homes and ate together with glad and sincere hearts, 47 praising God and enjoying the favor of all the people. And the Lord added to their number daily those who were being saved. (Acts 2:42–47)

7. Cleansing

> Jesus said, "A person who has bathed all over does not need to wash, except for the feet, to be entirely clean." (John 13:10, NLT)

A paraphrase of that verse might help to make more sense of it:

> *"A person who has received God's complete forgiveness by trusting Jesus is regarded by him as entirely clean. But he is bound to stumble at times as he conducts his daily business in this dirty world littered with spiritual potholes, so some of its filth will inevitably adhere to him. He doesn't then need to be completely re-bathed; he only needs me to wash the soiled part of him, which I am always glad to do."* (John 13:10, Paraphrase)

> 1 If anyone sins, we have an advocate who pleads our case before the Father. He is Jesus Christ, the one who is truly righteous.... 2 He himself is the sacrifice that atones for our sins.... (1 John 2:1b–2a, NLT)

We can't help but get dirty while trekking through this world. Even **saints** say and do things they shouldn't. But when we do, Jesus re-washes us in order to keep things fresh in our relationship with God. We only need to admit how we're wrong and reset our heart on loving him in order to clear the air. If we *don't* do that right away, our sin will start to stink like forgotten leftovers in a hot car. Things between us and the Spirit will turn sour and he won't drop the issue until we deal with it. We therefore need to keep this prayer handy and use it frequently:

*Believe it or not, you are now a "**saint**" in God's opinion! That's true of everyone he has called and cleansed. It means you have been "set apart for God" and are now regarded by him as holy and sacred.*

> 23 Search me, O God, and know my heart; test me and know my anxious thoughts. 24 Point out anything in me that offends you, and lead me along the path of everlasting life. (Psalm 139:23–24, NLT)

Q21: Does anything come to mind when you pray like that? If so, what do you think God wants you to do about it? Does anyone besides him deserve an apology or amends?

8. Communion

For two thousand years Christians have been using some of their time together to thoughtfully re-enact the "Lord's Supper," often as part of a shared meal. It is a graphic way to remind our faith of the ultimate price Jesus paid to secure the forgiveness and cleansing we need to be reconciled with God for all eternity.

> [23] … On the night when he was betrayed, the Lord Jesus took some bread [24] and gave thanks to God for it. Then he broke it in pieces and said, "This is my body, which is given for you. Do this in remembrance of me." [25] In the same way, he took the cup of wine after supper, saying, "This cup is the new covenant between God and his people—an agreement confirmed with my blood. Do this in remembrance of me as often as you drink it." (1 Corinthians 11:23b–25, NLT)

SECTION RECAP

Everything discussed in this section on **Obedience** is based on believing that...

1. God truly deserves it and welcomes it as an expression of our love for him.

2. We cannot dependably give it to him without considerable effort *and* supernatural assistance.

3. God's supernatural assistance is most available when our efforts to obey him include things like:

- **Resting Assured in His Love** – Chapter 11
- **Humbly Submitting to Jesus's Authority** – Chapter 12
- **Getting Familiar with God's Will** – Chapter 13
- **Focusing on Progress More than Perfection** – Chapter 14
- **Expecting Some Fierce Opposition** – Chapter 15
- **Cooperating with the Holy Spirit** – Chapter 16

Q22: Which one or two of those "activities" do you currently need to focus on most, and why?

We also identified eight resources we can turn to and rely on to help us "stay filled" with the indwelling Spirit of God so that his guidance and power are more readily accessible to us:

1. Music	3. Serving	5. Prayer	7. Cleansing
2. Thanksgiving	4. Scripture	6. Fellowship	8. Communion

Think of these as spiritual "power-ups." Using them is how we "feed the right dog" and get more of what we need from the Spirit to live in loving obedience. Better yet, think of them as ways to draw nearer to God and bask in his wonderful, transforming presence. They are meant to be used as *means* to that end.

Q23: How can you tell when you need to pay more attention to staying filled with the Spirit? What are some telltale signs that you're getting spiritually depleted?

POSSIBLE ANSWERS:

- *When very little of the "fruit of the Spirit" is evident in you. Re-read Galatians 5:22-23.*
- *When you frequently find yourself thinking, feeling or wanting things you know aren't good.*
- *When what sloshes out of you if you get "bumped" isn't pretty. Your attitude is lousy.*
- *When you know you're tolerating, watching, listening to or engaged in things that dishonor God, but you don't quickly end them.*
- *When you don't feel like spending time with God and aren't as interested in spiritual things. Your desire is diminished.*
- *When one or more of your relationships is strained or distant because of the above.*

Q24: Which of the eight "power-ups" do you need to rely on much more often, and how will you do so?

After you've decided on a couple, you then have to figure out how to wedge them in with all the other stuff that hogs your bandwidth. You'll probably have to give up a few *good* things, at least partially, because they affect you too much like eating chocolates before a nice meal. And you may have become too much like the conscientious lady in this story:

> 38 (Jesus) came to a village where a woman named Martha opened her home to him. 39 She had a sister called Mary, who sat at the Lord's feet listening to what he said. 40 But Martha was distracted by all the preparations that had to be made. She came to him and asked, "Lord, don't you care that my sister has left me to do the work by myself? Tell her to help me!" 41 "Martha, Martha," the Lord answered, "you are worried and upset about many things, 42 but few things are needed—or indeed only one. Mary has chosen what is better, and it will not be taken away from her." (Luke 10:38–42)

Q25: So what do you think Martha should have done?

Q26: What two or three things consistently hinder you from doing enough to stay filled with the Spirit, and what can you do about them?

Loving God by DELIGHTING IN Him

Few things make a parent's heart happier than making their child happy. That's what God is always trying to do with us, so then we *and* he can be blessed.

CHAPTER 17
DISCOVERING DELIGHT

Luke 17 tells a sad story about a miraculous healing. First some context. If you lived under the Law of Moses and contracted a certain kind of skin disease (like leprosy), your life could become painful and lonely really fast.[41] Not only did you look and feel (and even smell) gross, you were also contagious and had to be quarantined—sometimes for life—in an isolated colony. If you got remotely close to an uninfected person, you were expected to announce that you were "Unclean!" to warn them of the danger you posed. You were even forbidden to worship in God's temple because you were ceremonially impure. It was a thoroughly awful experience.

Ten men who shared that affliction heard of Jesus's ability to heal, so when he arrived one day on the outskirts of their village, they shouted to him from a distance and pleaded with him to do what only God could.

> 13 ... "Jesus, Master, have pity on us!" 14 When he saw them, he said, "Go, show yourselves to the priests. ..." (Luke 17:13b–14a)

That's what God's Law instructed you to do if your skin disease was apparently cured. Theirs didn't yet appear to be, but they decided to trust Jesus and do what they were told. Verse 14 tells us that "as they went, they were cleansed." Incredible! And then something odd happened.

> 15 One of them, when he saw he was healed, came back, praising God in a loud voice. 16 He threw himself at Jesus's feet and thanked him—and he was a Samaritan [usually treated with contempt as a spiritual outsider by the Jews]. 17 Jesus asked, "Were not all ten cleansed? Where are the other nine? 18 Has no one returned to give praise to God except this foreigner?" (Luke 17:15–18)

It sounds like more than Jesus's curiosity asking those questions—more like surprise and disappointment. And why bother to ask them out loud?

Probably because he was seizing a teachable moment to stress something we all need to hear.

---

[41] Historical records are not entirely consistent, so we're not positive that everyone with those skin conditions was treated the same way. But many of them were, and the ten men in Luke's story had banded together for a reason. The fact that they were all crying out for Jesus to show them mercy indicates they were badly hurting and more than a little desperate.

When God does us a big favor, it is dishonoring and disappointing to him when we don't respond with heartfelt appreciation—a missed opportunity for a closer bond with him. He doesn't merely intend for us to experience his love, but to reciprocate it. And not just in a "supposed-to," serious or dutiful way, but because we feel thrilled and blessed by him.

Notice again how Jesus phrased what he wants most of all:

> "Love the Lord your God with all your heart and with all your soul and with all your mind and with all your strength." (Mark 12:30)

That's still the big idea behind a fourth recurring theme in Scripture and the topic of this Section.

> My soul will rejoice in the LORD and delight in his salvation. (Psalm 35:9)

> Let all who take refuge in you be glad; let them ever sing for joy. Spread your protection over them, that those who love your name may rejoice in you. (Psalm 5:11)

> I will be glad and rejoice in you; I will sing the praises of your name, O Most High. (Psalm 9:2)

> [15] Blessed are those who have learned to acclaim you, who walk in the light of your presence, LORD. [16] They rejoice in your name all day long; they celebrate your righteousness. (Psalm 89:15–16)

> Rejoice in the Lord always. I will say it again: Rejoice! (Philippians 4:4)

> Delight yourself in the LORD, and he will give you the desires of your heart. (Psalm 37:4)

Rejoicing in the Lord is essentially the same as delighting in him and is one of the six most meaningful ways available to express our love for him. A closer analysis suggests that it's a blend of three simple activities that we can control and get better at with practice: (1) Noticing What's Good; (2) Reflecting on the Giver; and (3) Responding to the Giver.

1. Noticing What's Good

I could have thanked my wife this morning for washing the dishes I left in the sink last night, but I didn't notice until later that she had done so. It was a small miss, but it reminded me that our life together is sweeter when I do see such things and comment on them. It also made me wonder how many good things God does for me each day that slip by unnoticed. Probably a bunch, and no doubt it affects the sweetness of our relationship, too.

One way to address this is to deliberately pause every once in a while to inventory what's good in your life. What's going well, making things better and giving you pleasure? Count your blessings. I love this example of a guy doing it well:

2 Praise the LORD, my soul, and forget not all his benefits—3 who forgives all your sins and heals all your diseases, 4 who redeems your life from the pit and crowns you with love and compassion, 5 who satisfies your desires with good things so that your youth is renewed like the eagle's. 6 The LORD works righteousness and justice for all the oppressed. (Psalm 103:2–6)

May I never forget or overlook a single one of God's blessings. (Psalm 103:2b, Paraphrase)

A friend of the writer C.S. Lewis emphasized one way to notice what's good that permanently enhanced his ability to find delight in the Lord. Here is what Lewis wrote to him about that:

> *"You first taught me the great principle, 'Begin where you are.' I had thought one had to start by summoning up what we believe about the goodness and greatness of God, by thinking about creation and redemption and 'all the blessings of this life.' You turned to the brook and once more splashed your burning face and hands in the little waterfall and said: 'Why not begin with this?'*
>
> *... "And it worked. Apparently you have never guessed how much. That cushiony moss, that coldness and sound and dancing light were no doubt very minor blessings compared with [great biblical subjects like] 'the means of grace and the hope of glory.' But then they were manifest [clearly visible right there before my eyes]. So far as they were concerned, sight had replaced [my need for] faith. They were not the hope of glory, [but rather] were an exposition of the glory itself.*
>
> *... "Pleasures are shafts of [that] glory as it strikes our sensibility. ... Its flash upon our senses and mood is pleasure. ... Pure and spontaneous pleasures are 'patches of Godlight' in the woods of our experience. ... This sweet air [of our pleasures] whispers of the country from whence it blows. It is a message. We know we are being touched by a finger of that right hand at which there are pleasures for evermore."[42]*

Q1: How would you summarize what Lewis was saying and suggesting that we should do?

POSSIBLE ANSWERS: Pay better attention to what's good and beautiful right in front of you. Be deliberate about it. Spend more time looking for it in nature. Frequently remind and train yourself to notice it rather than letting so much pass by and taking it for granted. God is always present.

---

[42] C. S. Lewis, Letters to Malcolm, Chiefly on Prayer (San Francisco, Harper One, 2017), 119, 121. I have added to these selected portions a few explanatory additions for the sake of clarity.

Q2: What in your life do you especially enjoy or find beautiful? How have you been blessed by God, and what do you have to be grateful for? *Write your answers in the first column, leaving the other two columns blank for now.*

NOTICE WHAT'S GOOD AND BEAUTIFUL - *How* God Blesses Me -	REFLECT ON THE GIVER - *Why* God Blesses Me -	RESPOND TO THE GIVER - How I Will *Reciprocate* -

The more we notice the myriad ways God is busy blessing and working on our behalf, the more often we will be able to enjoy and appreciate them. That will then make it easier for us to enjoy and appreciate *him*, which is the second ingredient of delighting in him.

2. Reflecting on the Giver

This second feature of delighting in the Lord involves purposefully focusing our attention on him so he doesn't get left out of the picture. He is always in it, seen and unseen, and he is ultimately responsible for every blessed thing we enjoy.

Every good and perfect gift is from above, coming down from the Father of the heavenly lights, who does not change like shifting shadows. (James 1:17)

God ... richly provides us with everything for our enjoyment. (1 Timothy 6:17c)

Much of the good we experience seems simply to be the natural outcome of being born into a good family or what we've earned through our own efforts. But somehow God is also behind and involved in it all. He manipulates and steers and redirects even bad things—including our failures—to bring about long-term benefits for us.

> We know that God causes everything to work together for the good of those who love God and are called according to his purpose for them. (Romans 8:28, NLT)

That is a priceless guarantee. But more than just feeling glad for it, we also need to fixate on why it's so. What is it about God that relentlessly drives him to treat us so well? <u>Underline</u> what you see as you reflect on some of King David's three-thousand-year-old answers:

> ⁸ The LORD is compassionate and gracious, slow to anger, abounding in love. ⁹ He will not always accuse, nor will he harbor his anger forever; ¹⁰ he does not treat us as our sins deserve or repay us according to our iniquities. ¹¹ For as high as the heavens are above the earth, so great is his love for those who fear him; ¹² as far as the east is from the west, so far has he removed our transgressions from us. ¹³ As a father has compassion on his children, so the LORD has compassion on those who fear him; ¹⁴ for he knows how we are formed, he remembers that we are dust. (Psalm 103:8–14)

> ¹³ᵇ ... The LORD always keeps his promises; he is gracious in all he does. ¹⁴ The LORD helps the fallen and lifts those bent beneath their loads. ¹⁵ The eyes of all look to you in hope; you give them their food as they need it. ¹⁶ When you open your hand, you satisfy the hunger and thirst of every living thing. ¹⁷ The LORD is righteous in everything he does; he is filled with kindness. ¹⁸ The LORD is close to all who call on him, yes, to all who call on him in truth. ¹⁹ He grants the desires of those who fear him; he hears their cries for help and rescues them. ²⁰ The LORD protects all those who love him, but he destroys the wicked. ²¹ I will praise the LORD, and may everyone on earth bless his holy name forever and ever. (Psalm 145:13b–21)

Q3: What do the good gifts that God showers on us tell us about him? In the second column of the chart above, write down some of what you just underlined in Psalms 103 and 145.

The more we reflect on that last question, the more our heart will fill with gratitude and endearment toward God. And we will become more resolved than ever to rejoice and delight in him.

Only one of the cured lepers did that, and it quickly overwhelmed him with Jesus himself. The other nine were also ecstatic about their healings, but for some reason they neglected to delight in their Healer. They got what they wanted, but it doesn't look like they gave him another thought. Loving and being closer to him wasn't what they really wanted. May our tendency to respond like them die a quick death by our own hands. Then we can add-in the third ingredient of delight.

3. Responding to the Giver

The one leper didn't make nearly as big of a deal over his miracle as he did over his Benefactor. He was filled past his brim with delight in the Lord, and he expressed it by making a scene, "praising God repeatedly in a loud voice, throwing himself at Jesus's feet and thanking him over and over."[43] Don't think for a moment that Jesus failed to cherish that. Few things make a parent's heart happier than making their child happy. That's what he's always trying to do with us, so then we *and* he can be blessed.

Another example belongs here. It's an almost-embarrassing story reported in three of the gospels about a woman who deeply moved Jesus's heart with her expression of adoration and appreciation for him.[44] It was inappropriate in their culture for unmarried men and women to touch, and it was startlingly immodest for a woman to uncover or let her hair down in the presence of any man but her husband. Even so...

> Jesus was in Bethany reclining at the table in Simon the Leper's home. Mary—the sister of Lazarus, whom Jesus had raised from the dead—came to him with an alabaster jar of very expensive perfume, made of pure nard, which she poured on his head as he was reclining at the table. She also poured it on his feet and wiped them with her hair. And the house was filled with the fragrance of the perfume.
>
> Some of the disciples became indignant and said to one another, "Why this waste of perfume? It could have been sold for more than a year's wages and the money given to the poor." And they rebuked her harshly.
>
> "Leave her alone," said Jesus. "Why are you bothering her? She has done a beautiful thing to me. The poor you will always have with you, and you can help them any time you want. But you will not always have me. She did what she could. She poured perfume on my body beforehand to prepare me for my burial. Truly I tell you, wherever the gospel is preached throughout the world, what she has done will also be told, in memory of her."

Q4: Why is that? What factors made Mary's expression of love so meaningful to Jesus, and is there anything about them that you can take to heart?

The number of loving ways available to express our delight in the Lord is limited only by our imagination and inhibitions. For example:

---

[43] In vv. 15–16, the Greek verbs "praising" and "thanking" both describe a repeated or recurring action.

[44] I've combined the accounts of Matthew 26:6–13, Mark 14:3–9 and John 12:2–8 so you don't miss any of the details.

We Can...	It Can Be...
Praise him – Speak of his excellence; express approval, adoration and reverence	Kept personal or made public
	With or without words
Worship him – Credit him as worthy; show him respect, honor, deference and admiration; "kiss his hand"	In private or in public
	Indoors or outdoors
Bless/Extol him – Eulogize and speak well of him; tell others about him and what he's done	At church or anywhere else
	Subtle or extravagant, small or large
Thank him – Express appreciation and gratitude for his many acts of kindness, mercy, and generosity	Quiet, loud or lit up on a billboard
	Praying, humming, singing, shouting
Glorify him – Acknowledge his splendor, majesty, dignity and high status ("highness"); adore him	With or without musical instruments
	Laughing or crying
Exult in him – Express great joy and pleasure because of who he is or something he's done	Eyes shut or closed
	Arms outstretched or relaxed
Exalt him – Celebrate and speak highly of him; hold him in very high regard	On your face, kneeling, sitting, bowing, standing or dancing
Magnify him – Call attention to his excellence	Spontaneous or planned
Sacrifice – Do something bold and "expensive" for him	In times of pleasure or trouble

Q5: What would be a worthy response to each of God's blessings/gifts that you listed on page 132 in Column 1 and to what you wrote about him in Column 2? *(Remember the standout leper.)* Write your answers in Column 3, make a note regarding when you plan to give them, then share with someone a few of your most meaningful responses from those three columns.

There was nothing apparent in Job's circumstances that he could identify as good. But he assumed by faith that something more was going on than met the eye.

CHAPTER 18
AN OLD TESTAMENT EXAMPLE OF DELIGHTING UNDER DURESS

One of the surprising and powerful things about "delighting in the Lord" is that it's possible to do even when our situation seems awful and God appears to be elsewhere. But it doesn't mean we have to swallow our feelings or paint on a smile.[44] What it does mean is portrayed in many of the Bible's most dramatic stories.[45]

Take Job, a godly man who was nearly decimated by a series of devilish assaults. In the span of a few minutes he learned that all ten of his children had been killed in a "natural" disaster, and all of his vast wealth (consisting of servants, fields and thousands of livestock) had been either murdered, burned up or stolen. And since that wasn't bad enough, soon afterwards he was "afflicted with painful sores from the soles of his feet to the crown of his head which he scraped with a piece of broken pottery as he sat among the ashes" (Job 2:7). Makes me wince.

His was not a situation where you'd expect to find someone dancing for joy. The severity of the losses nearly wrecked that poor man. But somehow they *didn't*.

> [20] Job stood up and tore his robe in grief. Then he shaved his head and fell to the ground to *worship*. [21] He said, "I came naked from my mother's womb, and I will be naked when I leave. The LORD gave me what I had, and the LORD has taken it away. Praise the name of the LORD!" (Job 1:20–21, NLT)

Though the devil was allowed to cruelly plunge him into an intense and prolonged grief (accompanied by lots of questioning and complaining in later chapters), his sincere response was still to *praise* God—the third ingredient of delighting in the Lord! How on earth could he do that? The answer is in his practice of its first two activities: *Noticing What's Good* and *Reflecting on the Giver*.

1. Noticing What's Good

First, even though Job was feeling devastated and confused, he managed to see God at work in and behind his horrific experiences. There was nothing *apparent* in them that he could identify

---

[44] The contents of this chapter should remind you of what we covered in Chapter 8 on trusting Jesus in daily life, because nearly everything discussed here is *also* an expression of faith.

[45] Consult the list of faith-giants in Hebrews 11 if you'd like to read some.

as good. But he assumed by faith that something more was going on than met the eye. He chose *not* to believe that he was at the mercy of the world or the devil, because *God* was in charge! He was not alone in the storm; God was there "in the boat" with him, and had been all along![46] So Job looked for and discovered ("noticed") a bit of good in what he was going through, and that is the first thing one needs in order to delight in the Lord.

2. Reflecting on the Giver

He then took it a step further by *deciding to believe* virtuous and noble things about the God who was allowing it all to happen. He concluded that God had every right to deal with him however he pleased. He owed Job nothing. Life was not playing fairly, but its Author and Overseer was sovereign, blameless and trustworthy. That's what "reflecting on" God led Job to conclude, and it happens to be the second thing we need in order to delight in him. The third is…

3. Responding to the Giver

All that remained was for Job to "respond" to God, and he did so by offering a sacrifice of pristine trust and praise from out of his pain. Add these comments to what he said in 1:21:

Shall we accept good from God, and not trouble? (Job 2:10b)

Though he slay me, yet will I hope in him… (Job 13:15a)

> *His praise was made possible by his perspective. He couldn't delight in his circumstances, but he could and did delight in his Lord! So can we.*

It's never effortless and rarely includes happy feelings, but it's possible to follow Job's example even when life can't get much worse. Like him, we get to choose what we believe about God. The faith and love we express by continuing to believe he's good produces an aroma that he finds deeply pleasing.

---

[46] These are among the facts (in Chapter 10, Supplement C) that we need to rehearse when grappling with trials.

EXERCISE: Answer these questions in the four-column chart below:

Column 1: NEGATIVE REALITIES — What are one or two negative realities in your life that you're having a really hard time with, and in what ways are they affecting you? *Write your answers for each one next to a. and b. in Column 1.*

Column 2: NOTICE — Can you see anything good about (or in spite of) the negative realities you just wrote about, or anything good that might result from them later on? *Write your answers for each one next to a. and b. in Column 2.*

Column 3: REFLECT — What does the presence of good things you see in your negative realities tell you about God that warms your heart and helps you feel confident about your future? (In other words, what are some wonderful things that are still true about God in spite of what's happening to you?) *Write your answers next to a. and b. in Column 3.*

Column 4: RESPOND — What do you think would be an appropriately appreciative, admiring or grateful response to God for each of the things you wrote about him in Column 3? *Write your answers for each one next to a. and b. in Column 4. Remember the one leper.*

NEGATIVE REALITIES	NOTICE	REFLECT	RESPOND
a.	a.	a.	a.
b.	b.	b.	b.

Those who merely want life to go well and people to be nice won't be pleased to learn that God is getting *his* way if they aren't getting *theirs*.

CHAPTER 19
A NEW TESTAMENT EXAMPLE OF DELIGHTING UNDER DURESS

By the time Saul (later called Paul) of Tarsus was abruptly ordered to stop persecuting and start following Jesus, he was already a radical religious zealot. True, he slammed on his brakes and flipped a U-turn once he realized he was speeding in the wrong direction, but it didn't diminish his innate intensity. It simply harnessed him to a new Cause.

The resurrected Jesus commissioned Paul to evangelize (mostly) non-Jews scattered over hundreds of miles around the Mediterranean Sea. It wasn't long before he was taking long journeys and effectively sharing the gospel wherever he went. A growing number of people hated his guts and wanted him gone, but his fervent love for God and people was death-defying. Nothing seemed able to slow him down or cool him off.

On one occasion in the midst of a riot outside the Jerusalem temple, some soldiers intervened and grabbed Paul just as a Jewish mob was about to finish him. After discovering that he was a Roman citizen with legal rights, they relocated him to a city about 70 miles away and presented him to the authorities there.

After hearing his appeal, the local governor agreed that Paul should be sent to Rome and tried by Emperor Nero. But he also hoped to squeeze the apostle for a bribe and curry favor with the Jewish people, so he kept him in custody for a total of *two years* before shipping him on his way. The journey then took several months, and once Paul arrived he was confined to an apartment and chained 24/7 to a Roman soldier for two *MORE* years.

At times he must have felt like a stallion with its tail tied to a post.

The negative realities in our lives can have a similar effect by how they limit our options, alter our plans, ruin our dreams, slap us around, drain our energy and keep dragging on. They can be incredibly boring, frustrating, disorienting, humiliating, painful and discouraging. *(Underline the reactions that apply to you and feel free to add a couple of your own.)*

Yet those aren't the effects they usually had on Paul. In his letters he shares frankly that he sometimes struggled and felt like the rest of us would. But by the time he wrote a letter to distant Christian friends who were worried about him, he appears to have mastered the practice of delighting in the Lord in spite of his misfortunes.

> ¹² Now I want you to know, brothers and sisters, that what has happened to me has actually served to advance the gospel. ¹³ As a result, it has become clear throughout the whole palace guard and to everyone else that I am in chains for Christ. ¹⁴ And because of my chains, most of the brothers and sisters have become confident in the Lord and dare all the more to proclaim the gospel without fear.
>
> ¹⁵ It is true that some preach Christ out of envy and rivalry, but others out of goodwill. ¹⁶ The latter do so out of love, knowing that I am put here for the defense of the gospel. ¹⁷ The former preach Christ out of selfish ambition, not sincerely, supposing that they can stir up trouble for me while I am in chains. ¹⁸ But what does it matter? The important thing is that in every way, whether from false motives or true, Christ is preached. And because of this I rejoice.
>
> Yes, and I will continue to rejoice, ¹⁹ for I know that, through your prayers and God's provision of the Spirit of Jesus Christ, what has happened to me will turn out for my deliverance. ²⁰ I eagerly expect and hope that I will in no way be ashamed, but will have sufficient courage so that now as always Christ will be exalted in my body, whether by life or by death. ²¹ For to me, to live is Christ and to die is gain. (Philippians 1:12–21)

I want to become more like that guy before I die. But I wonder. Is it even *possible* to be, or was he totally unique as an apostle of Christ?

> *I remember being disappointed as a kid to learn that Superman couldn't share his superpowers with others. But Paul both could and did!*

He didn't just show off his ability to be joyful in adversity; he purposefully described what *made* him so in ways we can apply to ourselves. The key was how he kept adding fresh doses of the right three ingredients into the mix of his experiences. Here they are again:

1. Noticing What's Good

Q6: What good things did Paul observe had been going on in his life? What was God doing that gave Paul pleasure, even as a prisoner?

POSSIBLE ANSWERS:

- *No matter how grueling things were, God had been with him and guiding his steps all along.*
- *God was powerfully using him to spread the gospel in spite of his limiting and difficult circumstances.*
- *Caesar's Palace (the one in ancient Rome) was buzzing with talk about Jesus because of Paul's persuasive interactions with so many of his guards.*
- *Other local Christians were becoming bolder to share their faith because of Paul's courageous responses to his situation.*
- *Even those proclaiming Christ to gain attention and power for themselves were being used by God to speak his Word.*
- *All in all, the gospel was making impressive headway in that huge metropolis at the heart of the Roman empire.*

2. Reflecting on the Giver

Q7: What did those good things tell Paul about God that filled him with peace and gratitude? In other words, what did he continue to believe about God in spite of how things appeared?

POSSIBLE ANSWERS:

- *God truly loved the many thousands of lost people in that pagan culture and wanted to make them his own children.*
- *God was determined to deliver the message about Jesus that they all needed to hear.*
- *God had been masterfully working behind the scenes for years in advance, setting up the events and making the connections necessary to finally get the message to them.*
- *God loved and trusted Paul as a faithful servant and would continue to use him in significant ways. His life was as purpose-filled and important as ever.*

Reflecting on facts like those greatly relieved Paul's personal suffering and filled his heart with joy. But ask yourself this. Do you think they would have the same encouraging effect on most people in similar circumstances? Would they on you? Somehow it's easier to imagine the majority of us saying things like:

"This is all fine and nice to know, but what about me and my needs? I'm not really happy."

"My life has been on hold and uncomfortable for a long time now; I've had enough."

"When are you going to do something about this and make things better for me?"

Why don't we hear comments like those coming from Paul? Because no matter what it cost him, he wanted what God wanted more than anything else. First and most he prized his identity and calling as a servant-son of God. His highest value and priority in life was pleasing his Lord and Savior. So learning that Jesus's fame was spreading and his "business" was booming thrilled Paul's soul like few things could.

> "I consider my life worth nothing to me; my only aim is to finish the race and complete the task the Lord Jesus has given me." (Acts 20:24)

By contrast, those who want what *they* want more than (or instead of) what *God* wants—who just wish life would go well and people would be nice—are not going to feel relieved or overjoyed to learn that he's getting *his* way if they aren't getting *theirs*. Right?

So, if we want to share Paul's "superpower" of responding with joy to adversity, we will need to settle on the same conclusions he reached[47]:

- Jesus is the exalted Lord and King over all creation who deserves every drop of our adoration and devotion.[48]

- He can be absolutely trusted with everything and everyone we care about.[49]

- Our chief purpose and highest privilege on earth is to love, honor and serve Him.[50]

- He yearns to rescue people from their spiritual lostness, to make them right with God and to have them spend the rest of eternity with him.[51]

- Nothing else we might treasure in this life comes close to what he has in store for those who put him first.[52]

> **Q8:** Can you fully affirm all of those statements? Are there times when you're less inclined to?

Once those big ideas become our core convictions, we will be better equipped to join Paul in adding the third ingredient of God-delight into the mix of our negative experiences.

---

[47] This should ring a bell, because it's the same thing as "rehearsing the truth" in Chapter 10.
[48] Philippians 2:9–11
[49] Proverbs 3:5–6; Isaiah 26:3-4
[50] Revelation 4:11; 5:11–13
[51] Isaiah 65:1–2; Ezekiel 33:11; Luke 13:34; 2 Corinthians 5:17–21
[52] Matthew 19:29; 1 Corinthians 2:9

3. Responding to the Giver

Q9: How did Paul outwardly respond to what he noticed, admired and appreciated about God and God's activity in his difficult life? How did he express his delight in the Lord?

POSSIBLE ANSWERS:

- *By bragging-on God to others, telling them of all the amazing things he'd been doing.*
- *By exulting in how the Lord was spreading the Gospel in both the palace and the city.*
- *By expressing complete confidence in how God would work out the details of his future.*
- *By feeling and expressing to others a complete readiness to die for Christ.*
- *By declaring his determination to continue rejoicing no matter what happened, and by exhorting others to follow his lead.*

4 Rejoice in the Lord always. I will say it again: Rejoice! ... 18 Yes, and I will continue to rejoice.... (Philippians 4:4, 18c)

"Always," he said. Please don't think that means it's possible to live a life of undiluted, uninterrupted joy on this side of heaven. It isn't, and Paul's writings reveal that even he didn't. Neither did Jesus.

There's a big difference between rejoicing in our circumstances and rejoicing in the Lord.

Some of our disturbing questions won't get answered until we meet him face to face. Many hardships must simply be endured, and many losses must simply be grieved. Those parts of our journey can be grueling and long. We are not only to weep, but to weep with those who weep.

In this world you will have trouble. (John 16:33b)

We must go through many hardships to enter the kingdom of God. (Acts 14:22b)

But they cannot *compel* us to surrender our confidence that God is with us, loves us dearly, is working his plan and will someday relieve our pain so fully that it becomes a distant memory.

27 ... How can you say the LORD does not see your troubles? ...How can you say God ignores your rights? 28 Have you never heard? Have you never understood? The LORD is the everlasting God,

the Creator of all the earth. He never grows weak or weary. No one can measure the depths of his understanding. [29] He gives power to the weak and strength to the powerless. [30] Even youths will become weak and tired, and young men will fall in exhaustion. [31] But those who trust in the LORD will find new strength. They will soar high on wings like eagles. They will run and not grow weary. They will walk and not faint. (Isaiah 40:27b–31, NLT)

You [need] not grieve like people who have no hope. (1 Thessalonians 4:13b, NLT)

What we suffer now is nothing compared to the glory he will reveal to us later. (Romans 8:18, NLT)

[4] He will wipe every tear from (his people's) eyes. There will be no more death or mourning or crying or pain, for the old order of things (will pass) away. [5] He who (is) seated on the throne (says), "I am making everything new!" (Revelation 21:4–5)

There are *always* reasons to rejoice/delight in the Lord. It's just that *Noticing* those reasons, *Reflecting* on the goodness of their Giver and *Responding* appropriately to him is sometimes an exercise of raw faith and mixed emotions. Only occasionally will it gush out of us with no effort. But it will always be one of the best possible expressions of our love for God, and he will always cherish it when we do. Take this opportunity to practice it again by repeating the exercise you did earlier using the same instructions.

EXERCISE: Answer these questions in the four-column chart that follows:

Column 1: NEGATIVE REALITIES — What are one or two more negative realities in your life that you're having a really hard time with, and in what ways are they affecting you? *Write your answers for each one next to a. and b. in Column 1.*

Column 2: NOTICE — Can you see anything good about (or in spite of) the negative realities you just wrote about, or anything good that might result from them later on? *Write your answers for each one next to a. and b. in Column 2.*

Column 3: REFLECT — What does the presence of good things you see in your negative realities tell you about God that warms your heart and helps you feel confident about your future? (In other words, what are some wonderful things that are still true about God in spite of what's happening to you?) *Write your answers next to a. and b. in Column 3.*

Column 4: RESPOND — What do you think would be an appropriately appreciative, admiring or grateful response to God for each of the things you wrote about him in Column 3? *Write your answers for each one next to a. and b. in Column 4.* Again, remember the one leper.

NEGATIVE REALITIES	NOTICE WHAT'S GOOD	REFLECT ON THE GIVER	RESPOND TO THE GIVER
a.	a.	a.	a.
b.	b.	b.	b.

Q10: What would you say your heart most desires or longs for at this time in your life? Write your answer first, then read the quote that follows as you conclude this section.

"Think how surely rest comes with delighting in God. For the soul will certainly be calm once it is freed from the distraction of various desires by the one master-attraction. Such a soul is as still as the great river above the falls, when all the side currents and dimpling eddies and backwaters are eliminated by the attraction that draws every drop in the one direction. It is like a stream as it nears its end, and—forgetting how it brawled among rocks and flowers in the mountain glens—flows with a calm and serene motion to its rest in the sea. If you will direct the entire current of your being towards God, then your life will be filled and calmed by one master-passion which unites and stills your soul."

"If only our will could be set free from our love of fleshly delights, it would reach out towards God as a plant growing in darkness to the light—and we would wish for nothing contrary to him. The fulness of God is eager to fill the soul whose desires align with his purposes and embrace him as its highest good. To delight in God is to possess our delight. Heart! Lift up your gates: open and raise your narrow, low portals, and the King of Glory will stoop to enter."

(*Expositions of Holy Scripture* by Alexander Maclaren; *Psalm 37:4. Modified for modern readability.*)

An Exercise in Delight – Let's practice one more time what this Section is promoting.

1. Review Chapter 17.

2. Set aside at least one full hour to do nothing but focus your attention on something wonderful, beautiful, heart-warming or amazing. Then reflect on the Genius, Power and Love who is behind those things and designed them to bless you. Finally, respond to Him with pleasure, admiration and gratitude in whatever way seems most appropriate.

3. If you are going through this book with a group, the next time you meet, share with the others some of what you experienced in that hour. It will be especially meaningful for them if you share in a way that enables them to catch a glimpse of what you got to see and feel. Your entire time together will be spent doing just this.

SECTION FIVE

Loving God by SERVING Him

Jesus on earth was God on a mission to repair the devastation caused by people's rejection of his ways. There's still a lot of work to be done.

CHAPTER 20
THE WHOLE WORLD IS ON FIRE

One of the dumbest criticisms ever directed at Jesus was that he sometimes healed people on the wrong day of the week. His critics were right about God designating the Sabbath as a time for us to rest and focus more on him. But can you imagine telling someone who is choking or drowning, "Hang in there, friend; I'll come back first thing tomorrow morning and see what I can do"? *Jesus* couldn't.

> In his defense Jesus said to them, "My Father is always at his work to this very day, and I too am working." (John 5:17)

Caring about us is one thing God *never* delays or stops doing.

> [16] ... On the Sabbath day he went into the synagogue, as was his custom. He stood up to read, [17] and the scroll of the prophet Isaiah was handed to him. Unrolling it, he found the place where it is written: [18] "The Spirit of the Lord is on me, because he has anointed me to proclaim good news to the poor. He has sent me to proclaim freedom for the prisoners and recovery of sight for the blind, to set the oppressed free, [19] to proclaim the year of the Lord's favor." (Luke 4:16–19)

That passage in Isaiah 61:1-3 also says he was sent to bind up the broken-hearted, to proclaim release from darkness for the prisoners and the day of vengeance on God's enemies, to comfort all who mourn, to bestow on those who grieve a crown of beauty instead of ashes, the oil of joy instead of mourning, and a garment of praise instead of a spirit of despair.

> God anointed Jesus of Nazareth with the Holy Spirit and power, and he went around doing good and healing all who were under the power of the devil, because God was with him. (Acts 10:38)

Jesus on earth was God on a mission to repair the devastation caused by people's rejection of his ways, starting with Adam and Eve. Reflect on each of the following Scriptures and summarize its description of the consequences they suffered for their disobedience. These remain at the heart of what's wrong with us and our world, and what we need the most help to overcome.

1. ¹⁶ The LORD God commanded the man, "You are free to eat from any tree in the garden; ¹⁷ but you must not eat from the tree of the knowledge of good and evil, for when you eat from it you will certainly die. (Genesis 2:16–17)

THE CONSEQUENCES SUFFERED BY ADAM AND EVE BECAUSE OF THEIR SIN:

2. Then the eyes of both of them were opened, and they realized they were naked; so they sewed fig leaves together and made coverings for themselves. (Genesis 3:7)

THE CONSEQUENCES THEY SUFFERED:

3. ⁸ Then the man and his wife heard the sound of the LORD God as he was walking in the garden in the cool of the day, and they hid from the LORD God among the trees of the garden. ⁹ But the LORD God called to the man, "Where are you?" ¹⁰ He answered, "I heard you in the garden, and I was afraid because I was naked; so I hid." (Genesis 3:8–10)

THE CONSEQUENCES THEY SUFFERED:

4. ¹¹ And (God) said, "Who told you that you were naked? Have you eaten from the tree that I commanded you not to eat from?" ¹² The man said, "The woman you put here with me — she gave me some fruit from the tree, and I ate it." ¹³ Then the LORD God said to the woman, "What is this you have done?" The woman said, "The serpent deceived me, and I ate." (Genesis 3:11–13)

THE CONSEQUENCES THEY SUFFERED:

5. [14] So the LORD God said to the serpent, "Because you have done this, "Cursed are you above all livestock and all wild animals! You will crawl on your belly and you will eat dust all the days of your life. [15] And I will put enmity (*animosity*) between you and the woman, and between your offspring and hers; he will crush your head, and you will strike his heel." (Genesis 3:14–15)

THE CONSEQUENCES THEY SUFFERED:

6. [16] To the woman he said, "I will make your pains in childbearing very severe; with painful labor you will give birth to children. Your desire will be for your husband, and he will rule over you." [17] To Adam he said, "Because you listened to your wife and ate fruit from the tree about which I commanded you, 'You must not eat from it,' "Cursed is the ground because of you; through painful toil you will eat food from it all the days of your life. [18] It will produce thorns and thistles for you, and you will eat the plants of the field. [19] By the sweat of your brow you will eat your food until you return to the ground, since from it you were taken; for dust you are and to dust you will return." (Genesis 3:16–19)

THE CONSEQUENCES THEY SUFFERED:

7. [22] And the LORD God said, "The man has now become like one of us, knowing good and evil. He must not be allowed to reach out his hand and take also from the tree of life and eat, and live forever." [23] So the LORD God banished him from the Garden of Eden to work the ground from which he had been taken. [24] After he drove the man out, he placed on the east side of the Garden of Eden cherubim and a flaming sword flashing back and forth to guard the way to the tree of life. (Genesis 3:22–24)

THE CONSEQUENCES THEY SUFFERED:

8. [20] Against its will, all creation was subjected to God's curse (*futility, randomness, purposelessness, out-of-control-ness*). But with eager hope, [21] the creation looks forward to the day when it will join God's children in glorious freedom from death and decay. [22] For we know that all creation has been groaning as in the pains of childbirth right up to the present time. (Romans 8:20–22)

THE CONSEQUENCES THEY SUFFERED:

9. (By Noah's day,) the LORD saw how great the wickedness of the human race had become on the earth, and that every inclination of the thoughts of the human heart was only evil all the time. (Genesis 6:5)

THE CONSEQUENCES THEY SUFFERED:

Now compare the nine summaries you just wrote with this overview:

- They lost their purity and innocence; they had never before felt self-conscious or ashamed, but now they were consumed with both.
- They lost their sense of loving closeness with God; they were now disconnected from him and in conflict with him.
- Their peace of mind was replaced with condemning consciences, anxiety and a fear of punishment.
- They lost their natural innocence and easy intimacy as a couple; hiding and blaming became second-nature.
- They became more despised and easy targets of the devil's hostility and rebellion against God.
- They lost their immunity to disease, decay and death.
- They lost Paradise. They were evicted from their lush, gorgeous, custom-designed home and banished to live in a much more difficult and uncooperative environment.
- Nature itself was knocked erratic and no longer functioned as predictably or safely as God intended.
- Evil took root in the human heart and was passed down like a toxic gene to all their children.

Q1: Which of those negative realities have you or your loved ones been affected by most, and how?

Q2: What good can it do us to rehearse and stay mindful of all these bad things?

It's the unrelenting and pervasive presence of realities like these that pleads for us to join God's efforts to lighten them for others. That's a major part of what serving him entails, and it's also a great way to live as though we love him.

Why don't you pray right now for God to intervene, overturn, redirect, heal and bring relief to those who have been badly affected by the negative realities you noted in your answer to Q1.

Christians are spread way
too thin around the world,
because not nearly enough
of us have taken God's plan
for us to heart.

CHAPTER 21
THE WORLD NEEDS GOD *AND YOU*

We are still reaping consequences from what the human race began sowing at its inception. But that *doesn't* mean our Maker is done with us or has abandoned us to suffer what we deserve. The opposite is true.

> 6 (Christ/King Jesus), being in very nature God, did not consider equality with God something to be used to his own advantage (or *"clung to"*); 7 rather, he made himself nothing (*literally, "he emptied himself"*) by taking the very nature of a servant, being made in human likeness. 8 And being found in appearance as a man, he humbled himself by becoming obedient to death—even death on a cross! (Philippians 2:6–8)

Notice that the role he adopted when he came to our rescue was not merely human, but *servant*. Menial, poor, dirty, painful and humiliating were not beneath His Majesty.

> The Son of Man did not come to be served, but to serve, and to give his life as a ransom for many. (Matthew 20:28)

It bewildered angels, it was so extreme.[53]

Only love could conceive such a plan, and it didn't end there. On the day he triumphantly returns in all his splendor to be adored by those who love him, here's how he plans to treat them:

> 37 The servants who are ready and waiting for (their master's) return will be rewarded. I tell you the truth, he himself will seat them, put on an apron, and serve them as they sit and eat! 38 He may come in the middle of the night or just before dawn. But whenever he comes, he will reward the servants who are ready. ... 44 I tell you the truth, the master will put those servants in charge of all he owns. (Luke 12:37–44, NLT)

The point is that he couldn't possibly be more attentive or committed to helping and blessing us. That's why he never stops working—even on weekends—to repair and relieve us from the remaining damage caused by the original couple's "fall."

---

[53] 1 Peter 1:12

Even so, something down here is obviously still missing or not working as it should. That's the message in this story told by Bruce Wilkinson in his amazing book, *You Were Born for This*.[54]

A few years ago our creative team was shooting a feature film in South Africa in the dead of winter. The story centered on a Zulu boy who became orphaned when his parents and relatives all died of HIV/AIDS. To survive, the boy left his village and took up a hardscrabble existence fending for himself on the streets of Johannesburg.

One bitterly cold winter morning our crew was scheduled to begin shooting at five o'clock on a particular street corner. It was so cold that production assistants had arrived early to set up tents with gas heaters where we could keep ourselves warm. We all showed up at the set wearing scarves, gloves, and heavy coats—not the attire that usually comes to mind when people think of Africa.

By the time I arrived that morning, several police cars were already there, emergency lights flashing. The film team looked as if they were in the depths of despair. I asked the director of photography what was going on.

"I can't believe this," he told me somberly. "Last night, right across the street, a homeless boy froze to death. They found him this morning."

I was stunned. Everybody was. Then, as we contemplated what had happened, the terrible irony set in. Here we were to shoot a scene about a homeless orphan, and right across the street a homeless orphan boy died).

Why on earth did that happen? Did God care less about him than the boy who got rescued? No; it can't be that. More likely is the answer that there simply weren't enough caring people around to notice him or provide him with a jacket. Many of life's worst problems are due to the fact that Christians are spread way too thin around the world, because not nearly enough of us have taken his plan for us to heart:

(Jesus) died for everyone **so that** those who receive his new life will no longer live for themselves. Instead, they will live for Christ, who died and was raised for them. (2 Corinthians 5:15, NLT)

*He never meant for us to be mere recipients of his grace and generosity. He always intended for us to be **channels** of them as his servants.*

[1] ... Jesus knew that the hour had come for him to leave this world and go to the Father. Having loved his own who were in the world, he loved them to the end. [2] The evening meal was in progress, and the devil had already prompted Judas, the son of Simon Iscariot, to betray Jesus. [3] Jesus knew that the Father had put all things under his power, and that he had come from God and was returning to God; [4] so he got up from the meal, took off his outer clothing, and wrapped a towel around his waist. [5] After that, he poured water into a basin and began to wash his disciples' feet, drying them with the towel that was wrapped around him. ...

---

[54] (Colorado Springs: Multnomah Books, 2009), 44-5. It is still one of the most provocative and influential books I've read.

> [12] When he had finished washing their feet, he put on his clothes and returned to his place. "Do you understand what I have done for you?" he asked them. [13] "You call me 'Teacher' and 'Lord,' and rightly so, for that is what I am. [14] Now that I, your Lord and Teacher, have washed your feet, you also should wash one another's feet. [15] I have set you an example that you should do as I have done for you. [16] Very truly I tell you, no servant is greater than his master, nor is a messenger greater than the one who sent him. [17] Now that you know these things, you will be blessed if you do them." (John 13:1b–5, 12–17)

He now looks directly into *our* eyes and makes an appeal that sounds something like this:

> *"Much of the world is in a terrible mess. People everywhere are lost and distressed. I'm committed to making things better until I return and finish the job. But there's an enormous amount of work to be done until then. Will you join me?"*

Once they heard that message, Jesus's apostles were proud to grab his baton and run with it as hard and far as they could. One descriptive "label" soon became their favorite way to identify themselves:

> This ... is how you ought to regard us: *as servants of Christ.* (1 Corinthians 4:1a)[55]

That is our calling as well, and accepting it is one of the best possible ways for us to express our love for him.

> ... What does the LORD your God ask of you but to fear the LORD your God, to walk in obedience to him, *to love him, to serve the LORD your God with all your heart and with all your soul.* (Deuteronomy 10:12)

For 1400 years in ancient Jewish culture, an option of last resort for poor people who couldn't make a living or pay their debt was to sell themselves and become a servant in another person's household. But because God looks out for the disadvantaged, he forbade their owner-masters to keep them for over six years. After that they had to set their servants free and send them on their way with ample supplies—except in one situation mentioned by the law of Moses.

> [16] If your servant says to you, "I do not want to leave you," because he loves you and your family and is well off with you, [17] then take an awl and push it through his earlobe into the door, and he will become your servant for life. (Deuteronomy 15:16–17)

That graphically illustrated what later biblical writers had in mind when referring to themselves and us as "belonging to God." We are owned outright; no longer in charge of ourselves or free to live as we choose; always on-call and (supposedly) ready to do whatever we're told.

> [19] ... You do not belong to yourself, [20] for God bought you with a high price. ... (1 Corinthians 6:19b-20a, NLT)

---

[55] Compare Colossians 4:7, 12; James 1:1; 2 Peter 1:1.

Living in a society where personal space and boundaries are sacred, where "me-time" is precious and no one wants to be told what to think or how to act, the idea of becoming someone's full-time servant may sound like a complete drag. Yet it's actually our ticket to the most rousing, satisfying and rewarding life possible. As Jesus said many times:

> Whoever wants to save their life will lose it, but whoever loses their life for me will save it. (Luke 9:24)

> 25 Those who love their life in this world will lose it. Those who care nothing for their life in this world will keep it for eternity. 26 Anyone who wants to serve me must follow me, because my servants must be where I am. And the Father will honor anyone who serves me. (John 12:25–26, NLT)

> My purpose is to give (you) a rich and satisfying life. (John 10:10b, NLT)

So *gaining* yourself and *giving* yourself away turn out to be pretty much the same thing. As you spend yourself on what matters to God, you become more of what he means you to be and, in the process, acquire more of what your *own* heart desires.

We are increased, not diminished, by letting go and giving much. Of course, the opposite is just as true.

CHAPTER 22
YOUR NOSE BELONGS IN GOD'S BUSINESS

God's favorite way of getting things done is through agents. Sometimes they're angels; for a short while it was Jesus. Now it's usually *us*! Ever since Jesus took his body with him back into heaven and sent us his Spirit, *we* are how he is physically present in the world (1 Corinthians 12:27). That doesn't just mean we get a front row seat to watch the greatest show on earth. It means we get to *perform* it! And every one of us has a crucial role to play.

That's what Jesus was grooming his disciples for in their three years together. He was apprenticing them to work in his Father's business. And he did such a good job, the end result turned out even better than they expected.

> (Jesus said:) "I no longer call you servants, because a servant does not know his master's business. Instead, I have called you friends, for everything that I learned from my Father I have made known to you." (John 15:15)

Calling them "friends" meant he thought of them as a special category of servants that was more on the level of "partners."

> *"The slave (servant) is no more than an instrument. It is not for him to enter intelligently into the purposes of his owner. His task is simply to do what he is told. But this is not the pattern of relationship between Jesus and his disciples. ... He has kept nothing back from them. He has revealed to them all that the Father has made known to him. ... He has taken them fully into his confidence."[56]*

They learned all about his values and strategies, his immediate priorities and long-term goals—everything necessary to ensure that his business survived and prospered. Once it sank-in that he was leaving town and entrusting its daily operations to them, they quickly adopted it and started working as though it was their own.

Partners don't punch a clock like employees who are sometimes on-duty and sometimes off. Nor do they restrict themselves only to doing "their job." They are always available and take the initiative to do whatever is required, acting as the boss himself would if he were in their shoes.

---

[56] Leon Morris, The Gospel According to John (Grand Rapids: William B. Eerdmans Publishing Co., 1971), 675-6

That's what God wants *all* of his children to become. He is zealous about destroying the devil's work by repairing the damage people still suffer as a result of the Fall. And now that he has explained his business to us in those terms, he invites us to stick *our* noses into it: to make *his* business *our* business. Not only to work *for* him, but *with* and *alongside* him. True love for him will gladly lead us to do this. So, here are some practical pointers to guide us in that direction.

Don't Underestimate Your Importance

Do you ever figure it's unlikely that God will use you because you're too ordinary and don't have much to offer—the right personality, skills, education, background or whatever? Maybe you feel you've been damaged or disqualified by some trauma or stain on your record like addiction, a moral failure or recurring weakness, a criminal record, lack of faith, being too young or old, mental illness or emotional instability, divorce, bankruptcy, backsliding, homelessness or you-name-what-else.

Every one of those deficits can be found in the biblical histories of now-famous men and women whom God used proudly and powerfully to make the world better. Many were liars, cheats, doubters, promiscuous, murderers, idol worshippers, odd, teenagers and seniors, rich and poor, strong and sick, somebodies and nobodies.

God is evidently pleased to work through any and everyone who will let him.

I've been amazed over the years how God has used so many of the experiences I regarded as "unfortunate" or "awful" to create opportunities, build bridges, give me insight and make me *more* effective in my efforts to serve him. Few can relate better to another's struggle than the person who has grappled and received God's help with their own.

> ³ Praise be to the God and Father of our Lord Jesus Christ, the Father of compassion and the God of all comfort, ⁴ who comforts us in all our troubles, so that we can comfort those in any trouble with the comfort we ourselves receive from God. (2 Corinthians 1:3–4)

> [God says to us,] "My grace is all you need. My power works best in weakness." (2 Corinthians 12:9, NLT)

Q3: What have you experienced, struggled with or been damaged by that enables you to relate and "qualifies" you to help some people better than others can?

Q4: What is wrong with the world, society and people that you are especially disturbed by or concerned about and wish you could help to fix?

Stay Close to Jesus

⁴ (Jesus said,) "Remain in me, as I also remain in you. No branch can bear fruit by itself; it must remain in the vine. Neither can you bear fruit unless you remain in me. ⁵ I am the vine; you are the branches. If you remain in me and I in you, you will bear much fruit; apart from me you can do nothing. ⁶ If you do not remain in me, you are like a branch that is thrown away and withers; such branches are picked up, thrown into the fire and burned. ⁷ If you remain in me and my words remain in you, ask whatever you wish, and it will be done for you. ⁸ This is to my Father's glory, that you bear much fruit, showing yourselves to be my disciples." (John 15:4–8)

"Fruit" refers to any kind of God-honoring change he produces within us or through our efforts to serve him.

The key prerequisite to steady fruit-bearing is to "remain (*continue, abide*) in him." That involves staying loyal to him as our first love, spending plenty of quality time with him, being a diligent student of his teachings and striving to conform every part of our life to his instructions. Those who do such things can expect God to work powerfully—both in and through them—to bring about eternally significant changes in the world and people around them. Those who don't, can't.

Q5: What kinds of fruit are evident in your life?

Q6: What kinds of fruit are missing or infrequently present in your life?

> **Q7:** What one or two things would help you and Jesus to be "closer?"

Present Yourself to Be Used

> *It makes a great difference whether I am the landlord of my own mind and body, or only a tenant who is responsible to the real landlord. If somebody else made me for his own purposes, then I will have a lot of duties which I would not have if I simply belonged to myself.*[57]

Someone recently told me he was finally ready to get serious about following Jesus. Then he added, "But I've been reading the New Testament and I'm afraid of what he'll ask me to do."

I get it. We don't really know. It *could* involve extreme heat, crummy toilets, eating bugs or getting harassed. But we're talking about serving the One who faithfully feeds wild birds, ornately adorns roadside flowers and promises to be with us every moment until the end of this age.[58] We *can* trust him.

So offer your earlobe to his awl. Every morning—and as you approach or enter new situations throughout the day, even on vacations and days off—declare your desire and readiness to serve him. Ask if there's anything he wants you to do. Be like the prophet Isaiah when he heard God ask aloud if anyone was available to go on an important mission. His immediate and enthusiastic reply was, "Here I am! Send me!"

> **Q8:** Do you feel any hesitation or anxiety about saying something like that to God? If so, what are you afraid he might want you to do?

---

[57] C. S. Lewis, Mere Christianity (New York: Harper One, 2001), 74 (slightly altered for readability)
[58] Matthew 6:25–33; Luke 21:12–15; Matthew 28:20b.

CHAPTER 23
MORE WAYS TO BE A PARTNER

Find Some Way(s) to Serve

In my first year of following Jesus I had a brief conversation with a seasoned man of God from my church:

> He: "Bob, you need a ministry."
> Me: "What do you mean? Like what?"
> He: "It doesn't really matter. Just find a way to serve the Lord."

It was life-shaping advice. I made a few calls and within days discovered a weekly opportunity to share my faith with incarcerated teenagers. It required several hours of every Sunday and felt neither comfortable nor safe, but it got me off the bench and into the game where I started to experience a new exhilaration.

There are innumerable ways to get-in on a similar experience. For instance, Jesus will one day commend his faithful servants for acts of service ("ministries") like these:

> 35 I was hungry and you gave me something to eat, I was thirsty and you gave me something to drink, I was a stranger and you invited me in, 36 I needed clothes and you clothed me, I was sick and you looked after me, I was in prison and you came to visit me. ... 40 Truly I tell you, whatever you did for one of the least of these brothers and sisters of mine, you did for me. (Matthew 25:35–36, 40)

In other words:
1. We are continually surrounded by pressing needs, but...
2. we will remain oblivious to many of them unless...
3. someone urges us to get busy serving God, and...
4. we actually set out to do so.
5. Once we do, he will arrange our "chance meetings," open some doors, and empower us to partner with him in fixing the world.

Do Your Job as Jesus Would

There's another side to this that my friend with the good advice didn't mention. We aren't restricted to doing "Christian ministries" in order to love God by serving him. It's possible to do it simply by the ways we conduct ourselves while at work and in our vocation. In our hearts we can do *everything* as his representatives if we want to. Biblical instructions aimed at first century Christian slaves and masters still largely apply to the employees and employers of our day.

> [22] **Slaves**, obey your earthly masters in everything; and do it, not only when their eye is on you and to curry their favor, but with sincerity of heart and reverence for the Lord. [23] Whatever you do, work at it with all your heart, as working for the Lord, not for human masters, [24] since you know that you will receive an inheritance from the Lord as a reward. It is the Lord Christ you are serving. (Colossians 3:22–24)

> [1] **Masters**, provide your slaves with what is right and fair, because you know that you also have a Master in heaven. (Colossians 4:1; also see Ephesians 6:5–9 and 1 Timothy 6:1–2.)

> Whatever you do, whether in word or deed, do it all in the name of the Lord Jesus, giving thanks to God the Father through him. (Colossians 3:17)

Dallas Willard decodes that last verse in terms of "learning from Jesus how to do your job as Jesus himself would do it."[58]

Q9: What are some good ways for Christians to serve God on the job and with their work?

POSSIBLE ANSWERS:

- *Think of God as your boss*
- *Be cooperative, diligent and dependable*
- *Be friendly and agreeable*
- *Don't cut corners or be satisfied with "good enough"; aim at excellence*
- *Seek your employer's success, not merely your own profit or comfort*
- *Be completely honest and fair*
- *Own and learn from your mistakes*
- *Refuse to participate in things that are wrong or hurtful to others*

[58] Dallas Willard, *The Divine Conspiracy* (San Francisco: Harper, 1997), 287.

- *Assist people who need a hand*
- *Show respect to those with authority*
- *Try to stay cool in challenging and pressured situations; apologize if you don't*
- *Be ready to graciously share God's love and truth when it's needed*

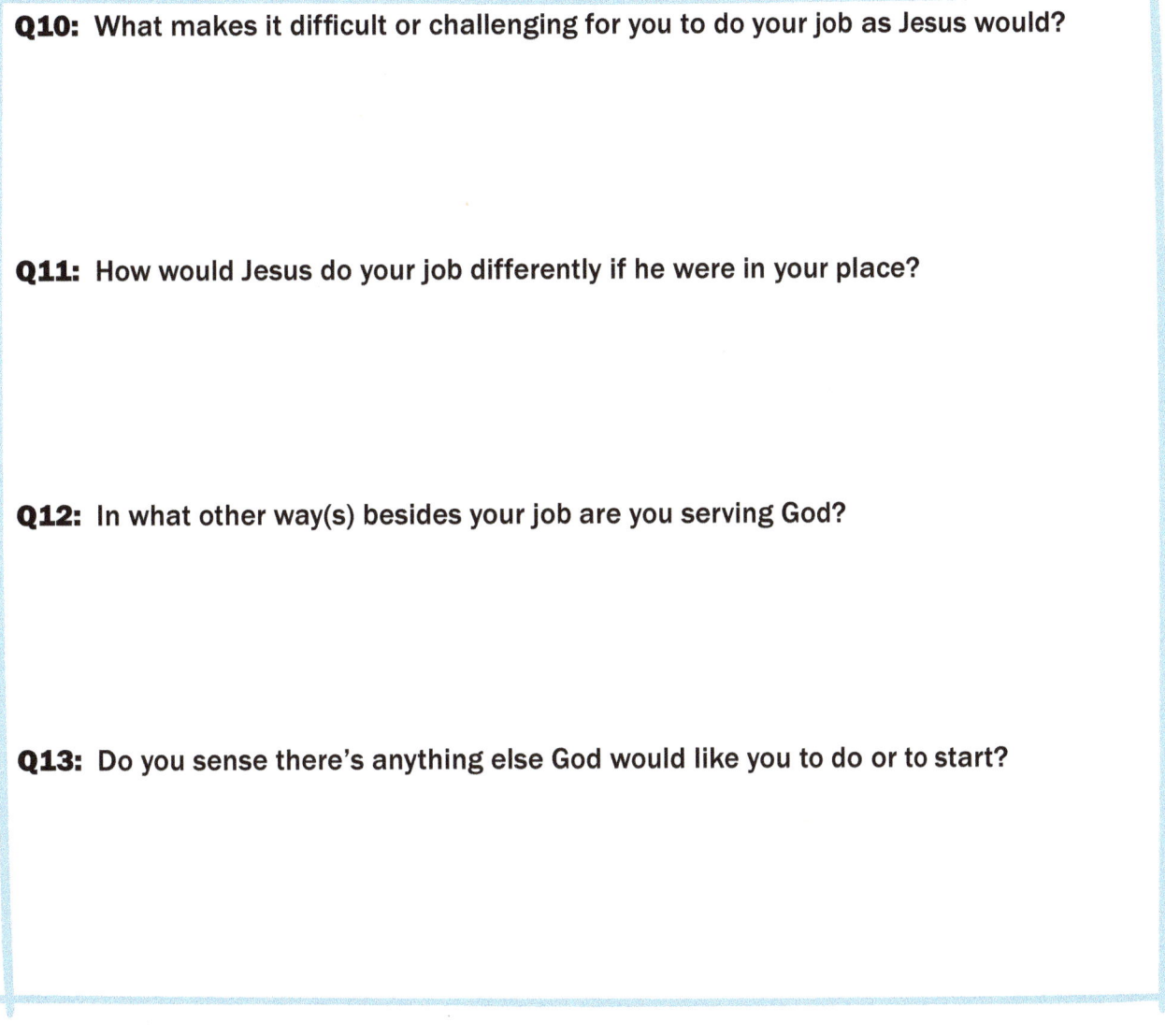

Q10: What makes it difficult or challenging for you to do your job as Jesus would?

Q11: How would Jesus do your job differently if he were in your place?

Q12: In what other way(s) besides your job are you serving God?

Q13: Do you sense there's anything else God would like you to do or to start?

Make God's Mission Yours

In the few days between his resurrection and ascension into heaven, Jesus never said anything like this to his followers: *"That was rough, but now it's over and we can finally say, 'Mission accomplished!' I've taught you everything you need to go back home and be successful. So have a good rest of your life and I'll see you again soon. Love you, bye."*

Nothing like that. What he did do was commission them with a fresh set of instructions on how to partner with him in the next stage of his worldwide rescue operation.

> 18 ... All authority in heaven and on earth has been given to me. 19 Therefore go and make disciples of all nations, baptizing them in the name of the Father and of the Son and of the Holy Spirit, 20 and teaching them to obey everything I have commanded you. And surely I am with you always, to the very end of the age. (Matthew 28:18b–20)

Those words apply to all of Jesus's followers, not just the original core. They pinpoint the focus of his main mission, the primary project he wants us to concentrate on until he returns: "making disciples (student-apprentices)." It essentially involves helping unbelievers reach a point of readiness to pledge their allegiance to Jesus, then helping them grow to full maturity in their faith. In his words there are three basic activities involved in this work:

- **Going** – Taking the initiative to engage in spiritually important conversations with non-Christians instead of waiting for them to ask or come to us.

- **Baptizing** – Publicly formalizing people's decisions to repent of their sins and become lovers of God by obeying his Son.

- **Teaching** – Mentoring those people to live every aspect of life as the Lord Jesus directs.

All of this is a way of re-saying that God wants everyone on earth to fully know his love and to fully love him back. But nothing like that will occur unless we who already love him adopt it as our mission. In this section we're highlighting that as one of the ways we can serve him. In the next section we'll talk much more about it as a practical way to love others.

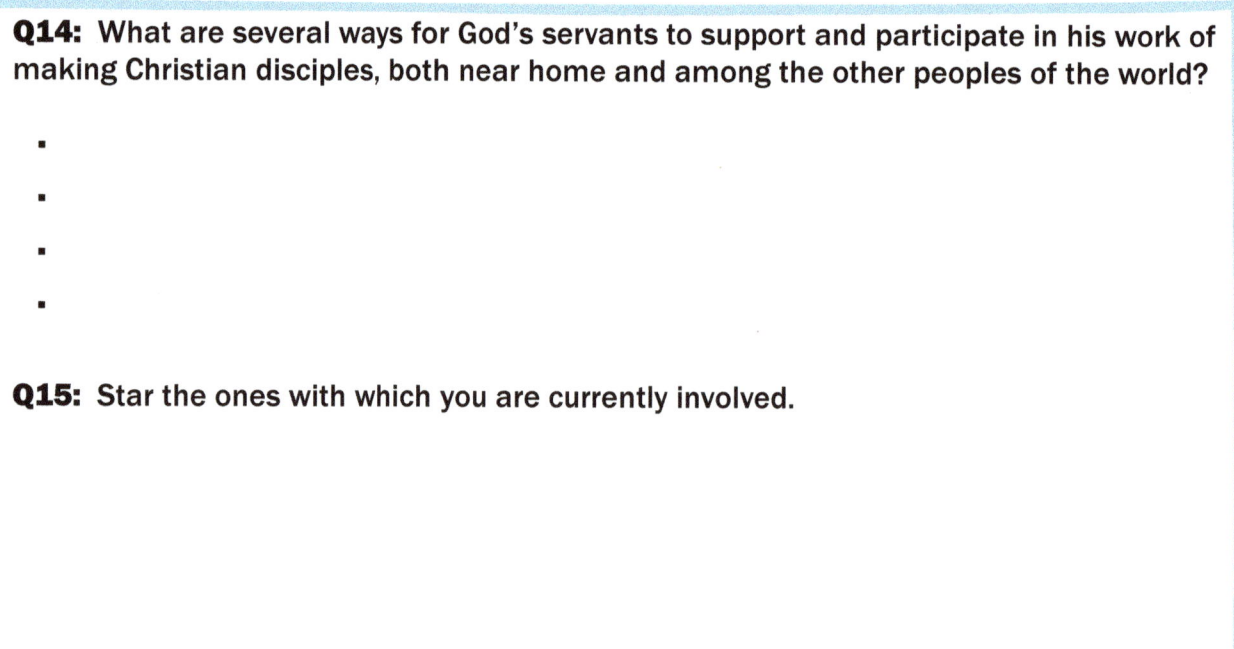

Q14: What are several ways for God's servants to support and participate in his work of making Christian disciples, both near home and among the other peoples of the world?

-

-

-

-

Q15: Star the ones with which you are currently involved.

Q16: Are there any that God might want you to get more involved with? If so, how?

Pray for Specific Results

After emphasizing our need to remain in him and for his word to remain in us, Jesus added a startling promise that we can "ask (God) for whatever you wish, and it will be done for you."[59] It may be unclear what-all that promise includes, but it's certainly a bold endorsement of prayer—both before and during our attempts to serve him. What he wants is for us to *partner* with him, and that's what our praying does.

The Bible is loaded with examples of God's people relying on him in prayer rather than just expecting him to do something. Paul entreated his friends to pray for him because he sincerely believed that vital things would happen if they did, but wouldn't if they didn't.

> [19] Pray for me, that whenever I speak, words may be given me so that I will fearlessly make known the mystery of the gospel, [20] for which I am an ambassador in chains. Pray that I may declare it fearlessly, as I should. (Ephesians 6:19–20)

I suppose that means Jesus in the Garden didn't receive everything he might have if his friends had prayed for him instead of falling asleep. Likewise, many since him have also had to go-without or wait longer for what they needed because their friends were preoccupied, snoozing or just plain lazy.

My former landlord Fern Keith lived to be 94. She used to wonder why God kept her alive after she became so feeble that she couldn't even leave her house. The single answer that made sense to her was that God wanted (needed?!) her here to keep praying for several things that especially needed his attention. So that's what she did.

*Prayer always, **always** makes some kind of a difference.
And specific prayer is more potent than generalized prayer.*

Jesus wasn't encouraging bland requests like, "Please help so and so" or "Bless the hands that prepared this food." He was inviting us to offer targeted petitions for particular changes and

---

[59] John 15:7

results that we know God desires because we understand his priorities. Praying for those is a vital piece of serving him in a way that accomplishes eternally significant results.

Q17: What does your normal practice of prayer suggest that you actually believe about prayer, and are you content with that?

Q18: What two or three things should you pray about more specifically?

CHAPTER 24
REMEMBER YOUR FUTURE

Sometimes the cost of joining Jesus and serving God includes being misunderstood, criticized, rejected or even attacked. Like when I dared to correct my mom's confusion about spirituality and she instantly went ballistic, pointing her finger in my face and furiously demanding that I never speak to her about it again. Or like when a joyful fellow I met in Ghana was severely beaten by his father and brothers after they learned he had converted from Islam. Jesus repeatedly tells us to not to be surprised by such reactions.

> 34 Do not suppose that I have come to bring peace to the earth. I did not come to bring peace, but a sword. 35 For I have come to turn a man against his father, a daughter against her mother, a daughter-in-law against her mother-in-law — 36 a man's enemies will be the members of his own household. (Matthew 10:34–36)

> 19 If you belonged to the world, it would love you as its own. As it is, you do not belong to the world, but I have chosen you out of the world. That is why the world hates you. 20 Remember what I told you: "A servant is not greater than his master." If they persecuted me, they will persecute you also.... (John 15:19–20a)

But that's not a typical experience for most of us. What it *usually* costs to serve God well involves more routine and daily things like...

- being loyal and loving to your spouse
- being present for your children and providing what they need
- being dependable, hard-working, cooperative and cheerful at work
- being really good at what you do
- being generous with your time and money in your church and community
- representing Jesus openly and winsomely with those who don't yet love him
- being at peace with everyone as much as it depends on you (Romans 12:8)
- maintaining a pure heart, a clear conscience and a sincere faith (1 Timothy 1:5)
- deserving a reputation for being kind, patient, reasonable, humble, honest and devout

All of these are important, but they can also feel like a *lot*. That's especially so when the people involved are difficult, there's too much drama, our load is increasing, the pressure is mounting, the problems keep recurring, the hole is getting deeper and we're not feeling our best or getting enough sleep. Since we're more vulnerable to feeling discouraged or fed-up in times like those, the Spirit reminds us:

My dear brothers and sisters, stand firm. Let nothing move you. Always give yourselves fully to the work of the Lord, because you know that your labor in the Lord is not in vain. (1 Corinthians 15:58)

God is not unjust; he will not forget your work and the love you have shown him as you have helped his people and continue to help them. (Hebrews 6:10)

The kingdom of heaven will be like a man going on a journey, who called his servants and entrusted differing amounts of his wealth to them, each according to their ability. Then he went on his journey. When he returns and settles accounts with them, he will say to each of those who put his money to work and thereby earned more, "Well done, good and faithful servant! You have been faithful with a few things; I will put you in charge of many things. Come and share your master's happiness!" (Matthew 25:14–23; *abbreviated to emphasize the point*)

Then the King will say to (them), "Come, you who are blessed by my Father; take your inheritance, the kingdom prepared for you since the creation of the world." (Matthew 25:34)

[2] Multitudes who sleep in the dust of the earth will awake: some to everlasting life, others to shame and everlasting contempt. [3] Those who are wise will shine like the brightness of the heavens, and those who lead many to righteousness, like the stars for ever and ever. (Daniel 12:2–3)

Q19: Which of the above reassurances most stirs your heart? *Underline it.*

Q20: When was the last time you needed reassurances like those, and why did you?

Maybe you don't need incentives like promises of future recognition or a fabulous inheritance to help you hang in there and keep doing the right thing. You serve God because you love him; he deserves it, you like to do it and people need it. That's terrific!

But if you find it even faintly encouraging to know that meeting Jesus in person will be the most awesome and joyful event of your lifetime, that he is going to acknowledge and reward your every act of faithfulness to him, then feel free to relish those thoughts as often as you please. It truly is going to be a great day and a huge relief.

> [17] Our present troubles are small and won't last very long. Yet they produce for us a glory that vastly outweighs them and will last forever! [18] So we don't look at the troubles we can see now; rather, we fix our gaze on things that cannot be seen. For the things we see now will soon be gone, but the things we cannot see will last forever. (2 Corinthians 4:17 – 18, NLT)

WRAP-UP: Two core thoughts have dominated this section on Serving.

- *Because he loves us, God is constantly working to repair and rescue us from the enduring consequences of our first parents' (and our subsequent) rebellion against him.*

- *Those of us who love him will devote ourselves to partnering with him in that work.*

The rest of the section then proposed seven ways to develop a true partnership with God:

1. Don't Underestimate God's Ability
2. Stay Close to Jesus
3. Present Yourself to Be Used
4. Find Some Way(s) to Serve
5. Make God's Mission Yours
6. Pray for Specific Results
7. Remember Your Future

Q21: Which of those seven do you need to focus on more, and how will you do so?

Q22: What conditions and realities in this world disturb, frustrate or sadden you the most?

Sometimes I'd like to ask God why he allows disasters, injustice and suffering to continue in the world when he could do something about them. But then I realize he could ask me the same question. [60]

Q23: If you knew God would work through you and bless your efforts, how would you most like to help people and make life better for them?

Q24: What do you think God might want you to do or try on his behalf, either now or soon?

---

[60] I decided to use this quote before I discovered that it was likely authored by Abdu'l-Bahá, a leader of the Baha'i faith. My doing so is not an endorsement of him or his religion; it's just a really good quote.

SECTION SIX

Loving God by LOVING PEOPLE

We need to keep reminding ourselves that we're on a mission and not here just to enjoy ourselves.

CHAPTER 25
THE PINNACLE VIRTUE

The ideas of loving God and loving people are permanently and emphatically coupled in Scripture.

> [21] [Jesus said,] "Those who accept my commandments and obey them are the ones who love me. … [24] Anyone who doesn't love me will not obey me." (John 14:21a, 24a, NLT)

> This is my commandment: Love each other…" (John 15:12, NLT)

> Whoever does not love their brother and sister, whom they have seen, cannot love God, whom they have not seen. (1 John 4:20b)

When Jesus spoke about our need to excel at this, he didn't add it last onto a list of six points. He elevated its importance to near-equality with loving God himself.

> [37] … "Love the Lord your God with all your heart and with all your soul and with all your mind. [38] This is the first and greatest commandment. [39] And the second is like it: Love your neighbor as yourself. [40] All the Law and the Prophets hang on these two commandments." (Matthew 22:37b–40)

The two together summarize all the other commands of God. *"All other duties will be done in doing these"* (Alexander Maclaren).

More than any of the other five ways to express our love for God, loving people separates the authentic followers of Jesus from the looky-loos and phonies. It should be what we are most vividly remembered for after we die, but I've attended over 100 funerals and it usually isn't.

> *Love is the most essential, life-giving gift we offer to another human being. It is also the least-likely, least-natural and least-consistent response that is offered, …[especially] during the difficult, soul-demanding struggles when we are threatened, reviled, and harmed. Rich moments of other-centered care and sacrifice are rare. Most people presume the desire to love is a natural human sentiment, but love is actually the exception, the extraordinary, and the life-altering surprise.*[61]

---

[61] Dan Allender, *Bold Love* (Colorado Springs: NavPress, 1992), 33–34.

C.S. Lewis reached the same dismaying conclusion on a more personal level in these first stanzas of his poem, *As the Ruin Falls*.

> *All this is flashy rhetoric about loving you;*
> *I never had a selfless thought since I was born.*
> *I am mercenary and self-seeking through and through;*
> *I want God, you, all friends, merely to serve my turn.*
>
> *Peace, reassurance, pleasure are the goals I seek;*
> *I cannot crawl one inch outside my proper skin.*
> *I talk of love—A scholar's parrot may talk Greek,*
> *But, self-imprisoned, always end where I begin...*[62]

I remember a sinking moment at the beginning of a pricey vacation in Maui with my wife and two pre-teen children. They were all tired, hangry, and complaining about one thing after another as we drove from the airport to our hotel. Suddenly an unwelcome thought popped into my mind: "I don't even like these people." I got over it by morning, but it wasn't nearly the last time I felt that way about someone I'm supposed to care for.

Loving people well is probably the most demanding part of following in Jesus's footsteps. Not because it's difficult to understand how, but because it's so hard to control our quickfire reactions and attitudes. Like descending on icy stairs without slipping, sometimes it's just impossible.

So let's clear up a common misunderstanding before we take this on. By telling us to "love our neighbors as ourselves," some think Jesus meant that we *can't* love others unless we first love ourselves. But that's not what he said. In fact, he was assuming that most of us don't *need* to make self-love a higher priority because we're already doing a fine job of it. We already care *plenty* about what *we* think and want and feel. What we need more is frequent reminders that our interests and concerns and preferences aren't always the most important.

> [3] ... Be humble, thinking of others as better *(more important and valuable)* than yourself. [4] Don't look out only for your own interests, but take an interest in others, too. (Philippians 2:3b–4, NLT)
>
> Sitting down, Jesus called the Twelve and said, "Anyone who wants to be first must be the very last, and the servant of all." (Mark 9:35)
>
> In everything, do to others what you would have them do to you, for this sums up the Law and the Prophets. (Matthew 7:12)

Eugene Peterson's *The Message* paraphrases the idea brilliantly.

> Here is a simple, rule-of-thumb guide for behavior: Ask yourself what you want people to do for *you*, then grab the initiative and do it for *them*. Add up God's Law and Prophets and this is what you get.

---

[62] C.S. Lewis, "As the Ruin Falls," in *Poems* (New York: Harcourt, Brace, Jovanavich, 1964).

That was already a "big ask," but Jesus then raised the standard still higher just before he headed to the cross.

A new command I give you: ... As I have loved you, so you must love one another. (John 13:34)

There is no greater love than to lay down one's life for one's friends. (John 15:13, NLT)

Q1: Who was the most loving person you've ever known, and what made them so?

Jesus was even *more* of what made that person so wonderful in your eyes. And *he* is who we need to become more like.

A Christian teacher once challenged me and several friends to do something for strangers that would bless them and stretch us beyond our current limits. Once he finished describing the uncomfortable assignment, he asked if any of us felt afraid. When a few of us nodded, he leaned in and said, "Then do it afraid." It still sounds like something Jesus would say.

The point is that we have to gear-up for this part of the game:

- to stop letting anxiety immobilize and silence us,[63]

- to let more offenses slide instead of getting so easily bothered or hurt,[64]

- to muzzle more of our negative, critical and opinionated ideas,[65]

- to keep reminding ourselves that we're on a mission and not here just to enjoy ourselves.[66]

Loving people as Jesus did is the best possible way to make God known and express our solidarity with him.

---

[63] The Spirit God gave us does not make us timid, but gives us power, love and self-discipline. (2 Timothy 1:7)

[64] Be kind and compassionate to one another, forgiving each other, just as in Christ God forgave you. (Ephesians 4:32)

[65] Do not let any unwholesome talk come out of your mouth, but only what is helpful for building others up according to their needs, that it may benefit those who listen. (Ephesians 4:29)

[66] 29 The time that remains is very short. So from now on, those with (spouses) should not focus only on their marriage. 30 Those who weep or who rejoice or who buy things should not be absorbed by their weeping or their joy or their possessions. 31 Those who use the things of the world should not become attached to them. For this world as we know it will soon pass away. (1 Corinthians 7:29b-31, NLT)

¹ If I speak in the tongues of men and of angels, but have not love, I am only a resounding gong or a clanging cymbal. ² If I have the gift of prophecy and can fathom all mysteries and all knowledge, and if I have a faith that can move mountains, but have not love, I am nothing. ³ If I give all I possess to the poor and surrender my body to the flames [of persecution], but have not love, I gain nothing. (1 Corinthians 13:1–3, NIV, '84)

In other words, there are people among us who express themselves beautifully in prayer, have unwavering faith in God and really know their Bibles. They are wise and insightful, zealous and bold, regular contributors and tireless workers who get a lot done. They stir hearts when they speak and may have thousands of admiring followers.

But **God** *is not one of them!* In his opinion, nothing they do or say matters, because they lack compassion and aren't truly interested in others' welfare. He loves them, but they won't be useful to him until they learn how to love.

When the Spirit speaks that bluntly, we need to pause and ask ourselves, "Is he talking about *me?*" Because if he is, though I may be a pretty good person, I still have some profound changes to make. The resurrected Jesus had especially strong words for his followers who were doing well in some areas but not so well at loving people.

² I know your deeds, your hard work and your perseverance. I know that you cannot tolerate wicked people, that you have tested those who claim to be apostles but are not, and have found them false. ³ You have persevered and have endured hardships for my name, and have not grown weary. ⁴ Yet I hold this against you: You have forsaken (*abandoned, given up, set aside*) the love you had at first. ⁵ Consider how far you have fallen! Repent and do the things you did at first.... (Revelation 2:2–5a)

Love is the pinnacle virtue, more honorable and precious than all the others.

...Make every effort to add moral excellence to your faith, and to your moral excellence add knowledge, to your knowledge add self-control, to your self-control add patient endurance, to your patient endurance add godliness, to your godliness add mutual affection, and to your mutual affection add generous love. (2 Peter 1:5–7 Paraphrase).

We won't get very far following Jesus unless we:

- adopt God's standard of love as our *own* ambition,
- learn to recognize what qualifies as love versus what *doesn't,*
- frequently acknowledge (to ourselves, him and others) our *failures* to love,
- then quickly refocus our aim back onto that objective and keep pressing toward it.

I Corinthians 13:13
Three things will last forever
—faith, hope, and love—
and the greatest of these is <u>love</u>.

Q2: If an invisible stranger followed you around every day for a month, what five or six words do you think they would choose to describe you?

Q3: How do you define "love?" What does it mean to "love" someone?

Q4: What does it take to become a more completely loving person?

"Being understood feels
so much like being loved
that most people can't
tell the difference."

CHAPTER 26
THE MAKE-UP OF LOVE - AWARENESS

The gospel writer Luke allows us to eavesdrop on a conversation Jesus had with a man who was struggling to accept the implications of God's requirement to love others. The poor guy felt so uncomfortable with it that he started looking for loopholes.

25 On one occasion an expert in interpreting the laws of the Jewish Bible stood up to test Jesus. "Teacher," he asked, "what must I do to inherit eternal life?" 26 Jesus replied, "What is written in God's word?" Jesus replied. "How do you read it?" 27 The man answered: "'Love the Lord your God with all your heart and with all your soul and with all your strength and with all your mind'; and, 'Love your neighbor as yourself.'" 28 "You have answered correctly," Jesus replied. "Do this and you will live." 29 But he wanted to justify himself, so he asked Jesus, "And who is my neighbor?" (Luke 10:25–29)

Q5: Why do you think that expert in Jewish law asked Jesus, "Who is my neighbor?"

Jesus delivered his response to our unloving attitudes in the form of a probing story with a kick for a conclusion. And in the process he revealed the nature of love.

30 In reply (to the law expert's question), Jesus said: "A man was going down from Jerusalem to Jericho, when he fell into the hands of robbers. They stripped him of his clothes, beat him and went away, leaving him half dead. 31 A priest happened to be going down the same road, and when he saw the man, he passed by on the other side. 32 So too, a Levite came to the place, and when he saw him, passed by on the other side. 33 But a Samaritan, as he traveled, came to where the man was; and when he saw him, he took pity on (had compassion for) him. 34 He went to him and bandaged his wounds, pouring on oil and wine. Then he put the man on his own donkey,

took him to an inn and took care of him. [35] The next day he took out two silver coins and gave them to the innkeeper. 'Look after him,' he said, 'and when I return, I will reimburse you for any extra expense you may have.'"

[36] Jesus then asked, "Which of these three do you think was a neighbor to the man who fell into the hands of robbers?" [37] The expert in God's law replied, "The one who had mercy on him." Jesus told him, "Go and do likewise." (Luke 10:30–37)

The *good* guy in this story is a Samaritan, but that's not how the Jews of Jesus's day would have regarded him. Samaritans were descended from Jewish ancestors who had broken God's laws by inter-marrying with pagan non-Jews. They lived together in a segregated part of Israel. They also refused to worship God in the Jerusalem temple and ignored all but the first five books of the Bible.

They were therefore scorned by most Jews as half-breed heretics, outsiders and spiritual rejects. A Samaritan was someone from whom you wouldn't expect *anything* good or godly. He certainly wasn't someone you would think of as a "neighbor" or a personal friend.

Q6: So why would Jesus choose a Samaritan to be the hero in his story instead of a respected "man of God?"

Q7: Who are the most difficult (kinds of) people for you to love as Jesus does? What are they like and what do they do that makes them difficult to love?

Q8: What do you tend to be like with those people instead of "loving?"

Re-read Luke 10:36–37 above and notice how Jesus answered the Bible expert's original question, "Who is my neighbor?" His point was that our neighbor is whoever happens to need us and be within our reach. You become a neighbor—or not—by how you respond to people and their needs.

But that's not all this story wants to teach. Look a little closer and you'll discover that love consists of three basic ingredients or working parts, each of which depends on the others to make it fully alive. These are the three essential components that love is made of.

The Make-up of Love:
1. Awareness → 2. Compassion → 3. Generosity

> *To love our neighbor as ourselves, and as Jesus loves us, requires that we:*
> **1. See** *their needs,*
> **2. Care** *about them, and*
> **3. Give** *them something to help.*

It's really practical when you break it down like this. First …

AWARENESS → Compassion → Generosity

One way God constantly demonstrates his love for us is by never taking his eyes off of us. He is watching and paying attention all the time. He *never* glances away or gets distracted. He knows and understands us completely, far better than we do ourselves.

> Hagar gave this name to the LORD who spoke to her: "You are the God who sees me...." (Genesis 16:13a)

> Your Father … sees what is done in secret. (Matthew 6:6b)

> Your Father knows what you need before you ask him. (Matthew 6:8b)

> Even the very hairs of your head are all numbered. (Matthew 10:30)

He is intimately acquainted with every moment of your history, and he knows every detail of what's going on in your present, both inside and outside of you. That's a large part of why God is able to love as well as he does. Awareness is love's first and most basic ingredient. Jesus mentioned it three distinct times in his parable:

> 31 A priest (religious professional) happened to be going down the same road, and when **he saw the man**, he passed by on the other side. 32 So too, a Levite (another religious professional) came to the place, and when **he saw him**, passed by on the other side. 33 But a Samaritan, as he traveled, came to where the man was; and when **he saw him** he took pity on him. (Luke 10:31–33)

All three of the main characters in Jesus's story had equal opportunities to love the man in need, because they all *saw* him lying there naked and bloody by the side of the road.

Love almost always "begins" by noticing a need, but people don't always wear their hearts on their sleeves. Their feelings, concerns and "issues" are at least partially concealed beneath the surface. So if we're to get better at loving, we first need to get good at discovering people's needs. There are many things we can do.

Seven Ways to Become More Aware

1. Assume

Nearly everyone is dealing with something difficult or carrying some kind of burden. Some are in our life circumstances, others in our souls. Examples include things like:

Trouble on the Outside	Trouble on the Inside
Marriage troubles/problems	Chronic pain, illness / Death
Trouble with children	Addiction (to drugs, alcohol, buying, porn, sex, romance, gambling, excitement, etc.)
Aging or difficult parents	Mental illness
Financial strains, losses, debts	
Unemployment	PTSD
Job pressure, instability, frustration, boredom	Sadness, depression, hopelessness
	Loneliness, insecurity, anxiety, fear, worry
Being misunderstood	Doubt, confusion
Being treated unfairly or unkindly	Disappointment, dissatisfaction
Abuse	Anger, resentment, frustration, bitterness
	Regret, guilt, shame, self-loathing
	Exhaustion, depletion, emptiness

Some of these troubles are more deeply rooted, complex and painful than others, but we share many of them in common at some point in time. **Go back and "star" the ones you *now* identify with most.**

Q9: What happens if people's troubles remain unresolved or their needs go unmet for very long?

Q10: How can knowing that we all share many of these same troubles help us fulfill our calling to love each other?

Again, the needs God wants us to care about in others aren't always *evident*. Even *they* don't always know what they need. So after we've made a few tentative assumptions, another way to become more aware of them is to...

2. Pray

Remember, the "means" God normally uses to meet people's needs is other people. *We* are how he's now physically present in our world. If we are going to love well in his name, we're going to need lots of help. Amazingly, so did his perfect Son!

> [15] The news about him spread all the more, so that crowds of people came to hear him and to be healed of their sicknesses. [16] But Jesus often withdrew to lonely places and prayed. (Luke 5:15–16)

Why? At least partly because he needed a continuous supply of perspective and guidance and fresh energy to ensure that he saw people and circumstances as his Father did and handled them as his Father wanted him to. One primary purpose of prayer "is to attenuate us to God's will and God's work going on all around us. If we ask God to show us what he sees, he will. And it will change us."[64]

Q11: What kinds of things should we be praying about and asking God for?

---

[64] Reggie McNeal, *Missional Renaissance, Changing the Scorecard for the Church* (San Francisco: Jossey-Bass, 2009), 70.

3. Observe

There are lots of reasons why more of us aren't more aware of the hurting, struggling people we're surrounded by. The most obvious is that we're preoccupied. We've got other stuff on our mind, too many things on our plate and a persistent electronic distraction in our hand. If we *truly* want to love people as Jesus does, we will have to regularly and firmly re-decide to pay attention to them.

Lift up your eyes and notice the ripe harvest all around you (John 4:35b).

Stop staring only at what's directly in front of you. Go into your day with your head on a swivel. Put away your phone and put up your antenna. Look more at people's faces and eyes and expressions. Notice their demeanor and what they're doing. Notice *them*.

Q12: What kinds of observable signs might indicate that a person is having a hard time or needs something in particular?

4. Engage

This activity goes a step beyond observing people to actually interacting with them in some way. Not necessarily with *everyone*, but with more than you normally do. Why? To discover if they need something that God could bless them with through *you*. Sure, some people will want to be left alone and have nothing to do with you. But many will appreciate being noticed and acknowledged.

We tend to send one of two basic messages to people when we see them. Either "Here I am," or "There you are!" The second one is like a skeleton key that opens all kinds of otherwise locked doors into people's hearts.

Q13: What simple things can we do to help us engage people?

POSSIBLE ANSWERS:

- *Don't just glance at or past them; look them in the eye.*
- *Smile. Say "Hi." Be friendly and warm.*
- *Comment on their appearance or demeanor.*
- *Try to enjoy them for a minute. Have a little fun with them.*
- *Wish them a great day.*

> I went out to find a friend, and nobody was there.
> I went out to be a friend, and friends were everywhere.[65]

5. Inquire

Be curious and inquisitive. Don't assume that their "real" need is the one that's most apparent. Probe a little. People tend to relax and find us much more interesting when we express interest in them. I've discovered that even strangers are frequently willing to share openly and personally once they sense we care and aren't trying to "sell" them anything (including our opinion).

Q14: What are some good questions we can use to help us know people better and deeper?

POSSIBLE ANSWERS:

- *How's your day going? What's been the best part of your day so far?*
- *It looks like you might be having a rough one. (Are you?)*
- *How are you holding up?*
- *How's your business doing?*
- *How is that (situation) affecting your faith? / How's your faith holding up?*
- *Can you tell me more about that?*
- *Did that experience damage or deepen your faith?*
- *You seem to have a lot on your mind. What's going on?*

---

[65] Adrian Rogers, from a 2019 sermon on Proverbs 17 titled, "The Friendship Factor."

An old acquaintance with a heart for God used to do some funny things. One afternoon he was walking the streets of downtown Santa Cruz, taking in the sights. He passed numerous people sitting on the sidewalks holding signs with nearly identical, hand-written messages: *"Homeless and hungry. Please help."* This provoked him to the point that he decided to return that night. He picked a busy, well-lit spot between a restaurant and a movie theater, sat down and held up a cardboard sign of his own for passers-by to read: *"Not homeless or hungry. What do YOU need?"*

He wound up having several interesting interactions with people, a few who offered him food until he asked them to re-read his sign. As it grew late, one person stopped and talked for 45 minutes about his ongoing depression, strained relationships and sense of purposelessness. They had a profound discussion about his hurts and God's love that ended in a tender time of prayer.

I understand that engaging more people and asking leading questions sounds awkward, even awful, to some in our ranks. They usually prefer to stay in their own space, mind their business and dabble briefly in light dialog. But bear in mind that you may have something people truly need (and will have to go without for now) unless you're willing to set aside your uneasiness and stretch-out a little in Jesus's name. Go back and "star" at least one of the above questions that you'd be willing to try.

6. Listen

...both to *what* people say and *how* they say it. Their choice of words and tone of voice may be tip-offs to something deeper, especially if they're being rude or unkind or vulgar. One of the best times to give people our rapt attention is when they're upset. What they're expressing feels *important* to them, and usually what they need first is someone to hear them out.

You don't have to like what they're spewing or how they appear, but if you can control your negative reactions and engage them kindly, perhaps God can use you to do them some good.

Q15: What are some of the worst mistakes that listeners tend to make?

POSSIBLE ANSWERS: Lack of eye contact; being distracted; interrupting; giving advice too soon, etc.

Two of the most powerful listening skills we can practice are (1) asking clarifying questions and (2) restating what we hear the person saying until they nod that we got it right. Using both skills together expresses a rare and powerful attitude that softens and opens people's hearts. "Being understood feels so much like being loved that most people can't tell the difference."[66]

> My dear brothers and sisters, take note of this: Everyone should be quick to listen, slow to speak and slow to become angry ... (James 1:19a).

God gave you two ears and one mouth. Use them proportionately.[67]

7. Divulge

By all means *don't* shift the topic off of them and onto you! But do help them see that you can identify with what they're saying. If you think it might help them feel less awkward, take a risk and disclose something of *your* experience, concerns, difficulties, weaknesses and struggles that are similar to theirs. Doing so can liberate others to be more open about themselves and their needs. Your expression of trust and vulnerability can make them feel safer and pave the way for a more personal and meaningful interaction.

Q16: What kinds of personal things (from the past or present) can you reveal about yourself that might encourage others to be more open about their needs?

CONCLUSION: One of Jesus's classic understatements is cited in John 16:33b: *"In this world you will have trouble."* For some people it's relatively short-lived and tolerable. But for others it can be acutely distressing, disorienting and depleting. Those folks, in particular, are the ones God wants us to love on his behalf. But in order to do so, we first have to be *aware* of what they're going through and what they need. Getting *good* at that is a perfectable skill.

---

[66] David Augsburger deserves credit for a similar quote in his book, *Caring Enough to Hear and Be Heard* (Regal Books, 1982).

[67] SIDE-POINT: If you're a person who *often* talks for a long while—over five minutes—before pausing and encouraging others to interject, you need to beat that bad habit. It's not just annoying and exhausting, it's unloving. And it's not how you (or God) want others to think of you. Do they *already*?

Give Me Your Eyes

Looked down from a broken sky
Traced out by the city lights
My world from a mile high
Best seat in the house tonight
Touched down on the cold black tar
Hold on for the sudden stop
Breathe in the familiar shock
Of confusion and chaos

All those people goin' somewhere
Why have I never cared?

CHORUS
Give me Your eyes for just one second
Give me Your eyes so I can see
Everything that I keep missing
Give me Your love for humanity
Give me Your arms for the broken-hearted
The ones that are far beyond my reach
Give me Your heart for the ones forgotten
Give me Your eyes so I can see
Yeah, Yeah, Yeah, Yeah

Step out on a busy street
See a girl and our eyes meet
Does her best to smile at me
To hide what's underneath

There's a man just to her right
Black suit and a bright red tie Too ashamed to
tell his wife
He's out of work, he's buyin' time

All those people goin' somewhere
Why have I never cared?

REPEAT CHORUS

I've been there a million times
A couple of million eyes
Just move and pass me by
I swear I never thought that I was wrong

Well I want a second glance
So give me a second chance
To see the way You've seen the people all along

REPEAT CHORUS

Give me Your Eyes *(Give me Your eyes for just one second)*
Lord, give me Your eyes *(Give me Your eyes so I can see)*
Everything *(Everything that I keep missing)*
That I keep missing

Give me Your heart *(Give me Your arms for the broken-hearted)*
For the broken hearted *(The ones that are far beyond my reach)*
Give me Your heart *(Give me Your heart for the ones forgotten)*
Lord, give me Your eyes *(Give me Your eyes so I can see)*

Yeah... Yeah...

EXERCISE: On three or four separate days this week, fill-in both Chart A and Chart B using these instructions:

> **FOR CHART A:** Try to become more aware of the concern(s) and need(s) of at least one person, using the methods discussed in this chapter. Then write down your answers to these three questions before the day ends.
>
> - **Column 1:** Whose concern and/or need did you become more aware of today?
>   *Note: "concerns" aren't necessarily the same as "needs." Try to discover both.*
> - **Column 2:** What concern and/or need did you became more aware of?
> - **Column 3:** How did you become more aware of their concern and/or need?

CHART A	1. Whose Need I Became Aware Of	2. The Need I Became Aware Of	3. How I Became Aware of This Need
Monday			
Tuesday			
Wednesday			
Thursday			
Friday			
Saturday			

> **FOR CHART B:** Also write your answers to each of these three questions:
> - **Column 1:** Whose concerns/needs did you **not** notice or become aware of today?
> - **Column 2:** *Why* didn't you notice or become more aware of them?
> - **Column 3:** What could you have done differently to become more aware of them?

CHART B	1. Whose Concern/ Need I "Missed"	2. Why I Didn't Notice Their Concern/Need	3. What I Could Have Done Differently
Monday			
Tuesday			
Wednesday			
Thursday			
Friday			
Saturday			

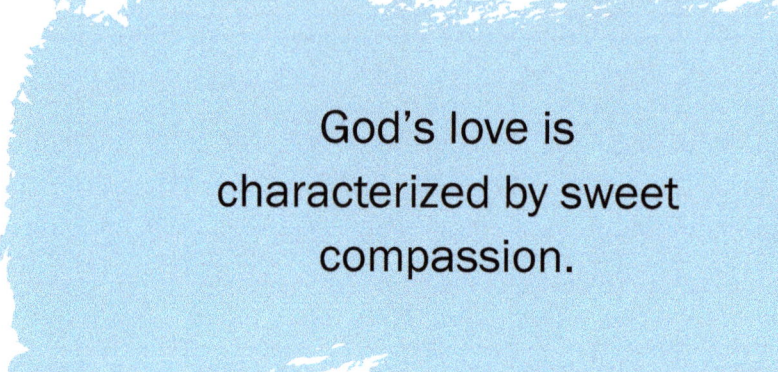

God's love is
characterized by sweet
compassion.

CHAPTER 27
THE MAKE-UP OF LOVE - COMPASSION

³³ A Samaritan, as he traveled, came to where the [bloodied victim] was [lying]; and when he saw him, he took pity on him. ³⁴ He went to him and (and then did numerous practical things to meet his needs). (Luke 10:33–34)

Q17: Compared to the previous two travelers, what was unique about the Samaritan and his response to the injured man?

The words, *"took pity on him,"* could just as well be translated, *"felt/had compassion for him."* The idea is only mentioned in passing and easy to miss, like a diamond in the dirt. But without compassion, nothing good would have transpired in Jesus's story. It is the second necessary component of true love.

*Awareness → **COMPASSION** → Generosity*

Compassion is one of the most beautiful and remarkable features of God's love for us. A synonym in Hebrew refers to the feeling a mother has for her nursing infant when it becomes hungry. It's the first word God chose to describe his own essential glory and goodness to Moses in Exodus 34.

God doesn't coldly tell us that everything is fine and to quit whining when we're in distress. He *feels* for us. He genuinely *cares* about what matters to us, just as any loving parent does for their child. Even when the trouble we're experiencing is our own fault.

The historical record of God's OT people is a centuries-long saga of suffering due to their recurring unfaithfulness and rebellion against him. But when at last they would cry out to him for help, he repeatedly responded by rescuing and restoring them. *The reason?*

> [22] The Lord's acts of lovingkindness never cease because his compassions never fail. [23] They are new every morning. Great is Your faithfulness. (Lamentations 3:22–23)

God's love is characterized by sweet compassion.

By the time of Jesus the Greek language had become universal; its word for compassion was spelled "splagchna." It sounds like what it means: "bowels" or "intestines." It refers to the part of us that gets moved or stirs when we notice another person's need or trouble. It's like empathy, but it isn't always something we *feel*. Notice how it's described here:

> If anyone has material possessions and sees a brother or sister in need but has **no pity** on them, how can the love of God be in that person? (1 John 3:17)

The idea of "having no pity on" a needy person literally means to "close your *splagchna* to" them. Picture it like this: every time you become aware of someone's need, the door of your heart pops ajar and provides you with an opportunity. You can either open it further to let them in, or you can pull it shut and go about your business. That decision is often made so quickly that you barely notice it, but you always get to choose whether or not you care.

The priest and the Levite in Jesus's story decided to close their hearts and keep on going. No doubt they had their reasons, but he left us to speculate what they might've been. Let's call them "Compassion Sappers." They are what stifle, deflect and extinguish our compassion before it has a chance to warm up and activate our generosity. Identifying them can give us a better shot at resisting and counteracting them.

Compassion Sappers

> **Q18:** If you had a chance to interview those first two travelers in Jesus's parable and ask, "Why didn't you help that poor fellow on the road?," what reasons or excuses do you suppose they might give?
>
> REASON/EXCUSE: SUMMARY WORD/PHRASE:
>
> - _____   _____
>
> - _____   _____
>
> - _____   _____
>
> - _____   _____

I'll bet our reasons are pretty similar.

Q19: What are some other reasons why people (and you) aren't always caring and loving in their (your) responses to others' needs?

REASON/EXCUSE:

SUMMARY WORD/PHRASE:

- *Eg.: We think they might deserve the trouble they're in.*
  Remedy: Don't presume or be so quick to judge.

  Judgmentalism

- *Eg.: We've been hurt or upset by them.*
  Remedy: Forgive as the Lord has forgiven you.

  Resentment; unforgiveness

- _____

  _____

- _____

  _____

- _____

  _____

- _____

  _____

Look back over your two lists, above (for Q18 and Q19), and put a "star" next to the reasons/excuses that most often keep *you* from being more compassionate. Then write down a good remedy or "counter" under each one of them.

What you included in those two lists is a pretty fair sampling of standard "Compassion Sappers." They are why we don't open the door of our heart to other people's needs more often. They are what block and distract us from being more caring and loving.

Surely God understands, right? All of us encounter more news of trouble and hardship than we could possibly have the capacity to care about deeply. Even so, many of our reasons and excuses for not caring are lame. That's partly why Jesus told the story of the Good Samaritan in the first place. He believes we *can* be more compassionate if we care to be, and we're not much use to him if we don't.

What Good Am I?

What good am I
If I'm like all the rest
If I just turn away
When I see how you're dressed
If I shut myself off
So I can't hear you cry
What good am I?

What good am I
If I know and don't do
If I see and don't say
If I look right through you
If I turn a deaf ear

To the thunder in the sky
What good am I?
What good am I
While you softly weep
And I hear in my head
What you say in your sleep
And I freeze in the moment
Like the rest who don't try
What good am I?

What good am I, then
To others and me
If I have every chance
And yet still fail to see?

If my hands are tied
Must I not wonder within
Who tied them and why
And where must I have been?

What good am I
If I say foolish things
And I laugh in the face
Of what sorrow brings
And I just turn my back
While you silently die?
What good am I?

Bob Dylan, "What Good Am I?"
on Oh Mercy, Special Rider Music,
Copyright © 1989

> **Q20:** What can you do to neutralize and counteract the things that usually sap your compassion?

I can think of three intentional counter-measures that are quite effective:

1. Become More Distractable

Nearly every moment, most of us are busy concentrating on something or headed to somewhere, so interruptions and distractions often strike us as annoying. But they don't *have* to. It's possible to view many of them as God-given opportunities to notice and care about people throughout our day. We can decide in advance to be more flexible and open to them if we'd like to be.

2. Follow Godly People's Examples

Years ago I invited a longtime friend to attend the Christmas Eve program at our church. He had never been there and didn't know a soul besides our family of four. When we four arrived a little late, we found him standing at the front doors, warmly greeting other people as they entered. You could say that no one really *needed* Dennis to do that, but he taught me a memorable lesson on choosing to care instead of keeping to myself and minding my own business.

> Here is a simple, rule-of-thumb guide for behavior: Ask yourself what you want people to do for you, then grab the initiative and do it for *them*. (Matthew 7:12 The Message, by Eugene Petersen)

You probably know someone who's really good at caring about others.[67] My kind and conscientious wife is absolutely one of them. God plants people like them to be fragrant examples and reminders along our path.

3. Frequently Refresh Your Connection with God

As already mentioned, one of our Father's best and most endearing qualities is his compassion. He is perpetually filled-to-overflowing with it. That probably explains why *my* heart feels more warm toward others after I hang out with him for a while. Something similar happened to another man who spent lots of extended time with God.

> [28] Moses was (on top of Mount Sinai) with the LORD for forty days and forty nights without eating bread or drinking water. And he wrote on the (stone) tablets the words of the covenant—the Ten Commandments. [29] When Moses came down from Mount Sinai with the two tablets of the

---

[67] Look back at your answer to Q1 in chapter 25.

covenant law in his hands, he was not aware that his face was radiant because he had spoken with the LORD. [30] When Aaron and all the Israelites saw Moses, his face was radiant…. (Exodus 34:28–30a)

You may be unable to set aside quite *that* much quality time to spend with God, but here's a promise you can take advantage of whenever you like.

Draw near to God and he will draw near to you. (James 4:8a)

Q21: What do your "quality times" with God consist of, and how do they affect you?

The point is that sometimes we won't have as much compassion available as people need us to. We therefore need to visit frequently and personally enough with God to have enough of his lingering warmth left over to share with others. Simple.

Since open-ended generosity is now the standard, *we* get to decide when and how much to give, not only with our money but with all the other assets and resources God has blessed us with.

CHAPTER 28
THE MAKE-UP OF LOVE – GENEROSITY

Through the OT laws and prophets, God commanded every Israelite to give him 10% (a "tithe") off the top of their earnings to support their priests, pay for their religious festivals and care for the poor among them. Failure to do so was "robbing God" (Malachi 3:12). Many churches and Christians continue to follow that instruction, but it is noticeably absent from the NT scriptures. The reason seems to be that God has introduced us to a "new" and improved standard.

> 6 Remember this: Whoever sows sparingly will also reap sparingly, and whoever sows generously will also reap generously. 7 Each of you should give what you have decided in your heart to give, not reluctantly or under compulsion, for God loves a cheerful giver. (2 Corinthians 9:6–7)

The amount we're now supposed to give in Jesus's name is however much "generous" is.

Awareness → Compassion → ***GENEROSITY***

Why would God set aside a simple rule in favor of a more general guideline left up to our interpretation? Because doing so appeals to our better motives. It also engages us with him and others on a more personal level, and it often encourages us to give more than we otherwise might. He's not seeking compliant robots but loving partners who are responsive to the spontaneous leading of his indwelling Spirit and able to read the needs of the moment.

Look again at how the Good Samaritan was a great example of one.

> 33 As he traveled, he came to where the (badly injured) man was; and when he saw him, he took pity on him. 34 He went to him and bandaged his wounds, pouring on oil and wine. Then he put the man on his own donkey, took him to an inn and took care of him. 35 The next day he took out two silver coins and gave them to the innkeeper. 'Look after him,' he said, 'and when I return, I will reimburse you for any extra expense you may have.'" (Luke 10:33–35)

Q22: In what ways was the Good Samaritan generous?

POSSIBLE ANSWERS:

- *He was quick to respond, probably because he was already inclined to.*
- *He changed his previous plans because he was open to being redirected.*
- *He showed disregard for himself and his own safety/welfare.*
- *He spent a lot of time getting fully involved with the person in need.*
- *He accepted responsibility for a stranger's well-being as a family member would.*
- *He thoughtfully paid attention to details.*
- *He was willing to get dirty and messy.*
- *He was unconcerned about the personal costs or getting reimbursed.*
- *He was willing to do with less and go without (by using his oil, wine, finances, donkey, etc.).*
- *He stayed concerned and involved until the need was met and the person was okay.*

Q23: Based on that loving man's example, how would you define "generous?"

Since open-ended generosity is now the standard, we get to decide when and how much to give, not only with our money but with all the other assets and resources God has blessed us with.

> [1] Now I want you to know, dear brothers and sisters, what God in his kindness has done through the churches in Macedonia. [2] They are being tested by many troubles, and they are very poor. But they are also filled with abundant joy, which has overflowed in rich generosity. [3] For I can testify that they gave not only what they could afford, but far more. And they did it of their own free will. [4] They begged us again and again for the privilege of sharing in the gift for the [poverty-stricken] believers in Jerusalem.
> [7] ... I want you to excel also in this gracious act of giving. [8] I am not commanding you to do this. But I am testing how genuine your love is by comparing it with the eagerness of other

(Christians). [9] You know the generous grace of our Lord Jesus Christ. Though he was rich, yet for your sakes he became poor, so that by his poverty he could make you rich. …

[11] … Give in proportion to what you have *(according to your means)*. [12] Whatever you give is acceptable if you give it eagerly *(willingly, not under compulsion)*. And give according to what you have, not what you don't have. [13] Of course, I don't mean your giving should make life easy for others and hard for yourselves. I only mean that there should be some equality. [14] Right now you have plenty and can help those who are in need. Later, they will have plenty and can share with you when you need it. In this way, things will be equal. [15] As the Scriptures say, "Those who gathered a lot had nothing left over, and those who gathered only a little had enough."
(2 Corinthians 8:1–4, 7–9, 11–15, NLT)

[10] Now he who supplies seed to the sower and bread for food will also supply and increase your store of seed and will enlarge the harvest of your righteousness. [11] You will be enriched *in every way* so that you can be generous *on every occasion*... (2 Corinthians 9:10–11)

It's just plain *smart* to be generous, and we can always *afford* to be!

Q24: With what kinds of things besides money can we be generous or stingy with others?

POSSIBLE ANSWERS:
- *Education, specialized training, expertise, experience*
- *Natural skills of various kinds*
- *Discretionary time to spend as you please*
- *Feeling good; having energy*
- *Being mentally sharp and verbally articulate*
- *A quick wit and good sense of humor*
- *Creativity and artistic abilities*
- *Being analytical and well-organized*
- *Knowledge of the Gospel and personal experiences with God*
- *Unique platforms and opportunities to interact with certain people*
- *A tender and sensitive heart*
- *Access in prayer to a loving and powerful God*

Q25: With which of the blessings/resources from Q24 (and any others you can think of) does God want you to be more generous? <u>Underline</u> them.

Right about now is when this topic starts to get more edgy and meddlesome. God wants us to be generous as he is, even when we don't feel like it and with people we don't especially enjoy.

> As we have opportunity, let us do good to *all* people.... (Galatians 6:10)

> Your Father in heaven...gives his sunlight to both the evil and the good, and he sends rain [for crops] on the just and the unjust alike. (Matthew 5:45b, NLT)

And this is how he instructs us to follow his example:

> [27] To you who are listening I say: Love your enemies, do good to those who hate you, [28] bless those who curse you, pray for those who mistreat you. [29] If someone slaps you on one cheek, turn to them the other also. If someone takes your coat, do not withhold your shirt from them. [30] Give to everyone who asks you, and if anyone takes what belongs to you, do not demand it back. [31] Do to others as you would have them do to you.
> [32] If you love those who love you, what credit is that to you? Even sinners love those who love them. [33] And if you do good to those who are good to you, what credit is that to you? Even sinners do that. [34] And if you lend to those from whom you expect repayment, what credit is that to you? Even sinners lend to sinners, expecting to be repaid in full. [35] But love your enemies, do good to them, and lend to them without expecting to get anything back. Then your reward will be great, and you will be children of the Most High, because he is kind to the ungrateful and wicked. [36] Be merciful, just as your Father is merciful. (Luke 6:27–36)

Q26: In your words, how would you summarize what God wants from us according to those verses, and why is it so important?

Based on the list of love's attributes in 1 Corinthians 1:3-10, here are some universal ways for love to be generous with all kinds of people. <u>Underline</u> the parts you need to get better at.

1. **Love is patient**, even when someone is irritating, annoying, frustrating, hurtful or difficult. Love is tolerant and slow to react when provoked.

2. **Love is kind**, even when someone is offensive, thoughtless, demanding, unappreciative or selfish. It responds with warmth, sensitivity, gentleness, sweetness, caring and tenderness, being careful not to offend, disturb or hurt people unless it's necessary.

3. **Love does not envy** or feel resentful if someone gets/has what you want (including attention, favor, things, opportunities, experiences, etc.). Love dislikes winning at someone else's expense, so it works for the good of others and is glad for them when they do well.

4. **Love does not boast**, even when you want to tell the world about your acquisitions and accomplishments. Love doesn't need recognition, status or applause; it actually enjoys stepping out of the spotlight and shining it onto others.

5. **Love is not proud**, so it rejects thoughts of being above, more deserving or better than anyone else. It regards others' interests, feelings and welfare as most important. It thus guides you to be open and gracious during disagreements, to admit when you're wrong and to give God/people credit for their role in your successes.

6. **Love does not dishonor others** but considers what is appropriate to the situation in order to honor God and show respect to people. Love cares about how others feel, so it is modest, discreet and careful not to embarrass, annoy or tempt someone to sin. Love is not rude or curt or sarcastic, but rather is tactful, pleasant, courteous and polite.

7. **Love is not self-seeking**, even when you feel like going first or grabbing the best for yourself. When others disagree or want something different than you, love won't let you demand that you get your way. It prefers to serve more than to be served, to listen more than to be heard, to understand more than to be understood. Love isn't concerned about your personal "rights," winning or what you "deserve."

8. **Love is not easily angered**, irritated, exasperated, outraged or provoked. It doesn't have a short fuse or thin skin, and it doesn't fight back. It makes you willing to take responsibility for your own attitude instead of blaming it on life or how people are treating you. It is good-natured and easy to get along with instead of touchy, reactive or defensive.

9. **Love keeps no record of wrongs**, even when you are severely hurt or offended. Love refuses to harbor resentment, nurse a grudge or grow bitter. It feels compassion and is quick to forgive. It overlooks people's faults and offenses rather than calling attention to them or making them pay. *(See Luke 6:36-37 and Matthew 18:21-35.)*

10. **Love does not delight in evil** or wrongdoing, and it doesn't find pleasure in another's misfortune. Love refuses to celebrate, enjoy or approve of what is shameful or displeases God. It doesn't relish discovering or criticizing what is wrong, though it is willing to confront and challenge it. And it feels responsible to work against the injustice and violence that oppress so many people in our broken world.

11. **Love rejoices with the truth**, so rigorous honesty is one of its highest values. Love persuades you to pay the price of keeping your word and staying loyal, even if it is expensive. It looks for openings to help others discover and embrace what's true. It delights to see injustices overturned and people honoring God by doing the right thing.

12. Love never gives up (NLT) or collapses under the weight of a burdensome relationship. When offenses, frustrations, demands or needs build up, love doesn't finally decide, "I can't take this anymore," and then quit. For love there is no hopeless case, so it bears up under strain, adapts when necessary and continues to support.[68]

13. Love never loses faith (NLT). It prefers to assume and believe the best about others instead of being suspicious, cynical or questioning their motives. Love is hesitant to believe a bad report about someone and refuses to jump to conclusions. Love inclines us to take people at their word and give them the benefit of the doubt.

14. Love is always hopeful (NLT). Even after learning that the best isn't true about someone, love still prefers to be optimistic about them and the "next time." Love confidently entrusts others to God and patiently waits for him to change them for the better.

15. Love always perseveres, because it believes in long-term commitments. People matter, so it is determined to finish what it starts with them. In spite of challenges, hardships, resistance, misunderstandings, hurt feelings, setbacks and breakdowns, love chooses to remain steadfast and faithful in order to outlast and overcome what threatens to undo it.

16. Love never fails. It is as long-lasting as God. It cannot ultimately be extinguished or defeated. Love is the gutsiest, strongest, most ambitious and life-changing power in the universe. And it always will be.

REFLECTION AND APPLICATION EXERCISE:
Read back over what you underlined above, and "star" a few (no more than four or five) characteristics of love that are *least* evident in your character or lifestyle at this time.

- In the 1st column boxes below, write down each of the items you just starred.
- In the 2nd column boxes, write down what you tend to be like **instead** of loving.
- In the 3rd column, write down **when**—and **with whom**—you need to be more loving.

How I Need to Love Better	What I Tend to Be Like Instead	When & Who I Need to Love Better

[68] Of course there are exceptions to this general rule when situations become extreme or staying with a person becomes dangerous or impossible.

CHAPTER 29
GENEROSITY WITH OUR FAMILY

God literally expects us to love everybody as he does! But certain kinds of people need our extra attention, so he directs us to concentrate on them even more than others. For example, we must be particularly generous with those who are physically and/or spiritually related to us.

With Physical Relatives

Anyone who does not provide for their relatives, and especially for their own household, has denied the faith and is worse than an unbeliever. (1 Timothy 5:8)

You husbands must give honor to your wives. Treat your wife with understanding as you live together. She may be weaker than you are, but she is your equal partner in God's gift of new life. Treat her as you should so your prayers will not be hindered. (1 Peter 3:7, NLT)

Husbands, love your wives, just as Christ loved the church and gave himself up for her... (Ephesians 5:25b)

4... urge the younger women to love their husbands and children, 5 to be self-controlled and pure, to be busy at home, to be kind, and to be subject to their husbands, so that no one will malign the word of God. (Titus 2:4–5)

Fathers [and mothers], do not exasperate your children; instead, bring them up in the training and instruction of the Lord. (Ephesians 6:4)

With Spiritual Relatives

As we have opportunity, let us do good to all people, *especially* to those who belong to the family of believers. (Galatians 6:10)

31 When the Son of Man comes in his glory, and all the angels with him, he will sit on his glorious throne. 32 All the nations will be gathered before him, and he will separate the people

one from another as a shepherd separates the sheep from the goats. [33] He will put the sheep on his right and the goats on his left.

[34] Then the King will say to those on his right, "Come, you who are blessed by my Father; take your inheritance, the kingdom prepared for you since the creation of the world. [35] For I was hungry and you gave me something to eat, I was thirsty and you gave me something to drink, I was a stranger and you invited me in, [36] I needed clothes and you clothed me, I was sick and you looked after me, I was in prison and you came to visit me."

[37] Then the righteous will answer him, "Lord, when did we see you hungry and feed you, or thirsty and give you something to drink? [38] When did we see you a stranger and invite you in, or needing clothes and clothe you? [39] When did we see you sick or in prison and go to visit you?" [40] The King will reply, "Truly I tell you, whatever you did for one of the least of these brothers and sisters of mine, you did for me." (Matthew 25:31–40)

Q27: What questions do those verses (in both of the above categories) raise for you?

Q28: Who in your family or God's family could fairly say that you haven't been as loving or generous with them recently as they need you to be?

Spiritual Gifts Meant Especially for "Family"

You may be unaware of it, but you've been given at least one divinely-enhanced ability to strengthen and care for your brothers and sisters in Christ.

[10] Each of you should use whatever gift you have received to serve others, as faithful stewards of God's grace in its various forms. [11] If anyone speaks, they should do so as one who speaks the very words of God. If anyone serves, they should do so with the strength God provides, so that in all things God may be praised through Jesus Christ. … (1 Peter 4:10–11a)

Paul was apparently referring to those abilities when he wrote about *spiritual gifts* and called them "manifestations of the Spirit" (1 Corinthians 12:7). They are unique ways that God internally directs and enables his people to meet each other's needs and help each other grow.

They are often experienced as an increase of clarity, insight, confidence, precision, energy, guidance, compassion or certainty regarding what God wants us to say and do next. Most of them empower us to achieve better results or a more profound impact than we would have expected. They can be grouped roughly into two categories. Read over them and see if any "feel familiar."[69]

SPEAKING GIFTS	SERVING GIFTS
Evangelism – a deep concern about people's need for Jesus, a desire to lead them to him and an ability to do so with clarity and power	**Serving** – helping out, contributing to and participating in tasks or projects to get things done
Prophesying – delivering a direct message from God intended to strengthen, warn, challenge, confront, console, guide or encourage	**Leading** – taking initiative, setting goals, making plans, organizing, supervising, delegating and guiding others to reach an objective
Teaching – clearly explaining and applying the Word of God	**Showing Mercy** – extending compassion and kindness; relieving others' distress
Encouraging – reassuring, challenging, urging, imploring or motivating to action	**Giving** – using one's resources to assist those in need or support a cause that God cares about
A Word of Wisdom – a well-timed message conveying insight, perspective, advice or guidance, usually based on Scripture	**Faith** – continuing to trust God and maintain confidence; envisioning goals and expecting God to provide what's needed to achieve them
A Word of Knowledge – a well-timed message conveying needed facts, information or answers, especially from God's Word	**Miraculous Powers** – mediating God's power to bypass natural laws or overpower devilish influences
Tongues – a full heart praying or praising God in a foreign or unknown language	**Healings** – mediating God's power to fully restore someone's physical/mental wholeness
Interpretation of Tongues – deciphering and/or explaining what was spoken in "tongues" so it can benefit those who heard	**Distinguishing Spirits** – discerning if it is God or some other source behind an idea, plan, action, experience, outcome or person

---

[69] Ephesians 4:11, Romans 12:6–8 and 1 Corinthians 12–14 are the most detailed lists of gifts, but they don't match each other and should be understood as partial. Solid Christians disagree whether all of the gifts listed are still operating, and some of the brief gift "definitions" provided here need further clarification.

Since the Bible doesn't provide full definitions of these gifts or a "test" to help us know which one(s) we may have, the best way to "activate" and become familiar with yours is to concentrate on caring for people and responding to the needs you become aware of. As you do, the Spirit will manifest his presence in and through you when he sees fit. And you will learn by experience how he prefers to use you in certain situations so you'll quickly recognize when to step-in and get involved.

The Holy Spirit can temporarily distribute any of several gifts to whomever He pleases according to the needs of the moment. But these verses **seem** *to say that He also permanently assigns at least one to every Christian for them to utilize and perfect over time:*

We *have* different gifts, according to the grace given to each of us (Romans 12:6).

Each of you should use whatever gift *you have received* to serve others, as faithful stewards of God's grace in its various forms (1 Peter 4:10).

[18] … *God has placed* the parts in the body, every one of them, just as he wanted them to be. [19] If they were all one part, where would the body be? [20] As it is, there are many parts, but one body" (1 Corinthians 12:18b–19).

Q29: Which of the spiritual gifts on page 209 describe how you're most inclined to respond to people and problems?

Q30: In what situations and with what people does God seem to use you most?

Q31: What does your last answer suggest about how he wants you to act in the future?

CHAPTER 30
GENEROSITY WITH THE DISTRESSED

[God's] people must learn to devote themselves to doing what is good, in order to provide for urgent needs …. (Titus 3:14)

Q32: What kind of needs deserve to be treated as "urgent?"

Look back in Chapter 26 at the two-column chart of external and internal "Troubles" that we can *assume* people have. From that chart, add the most "urgent" ones to your answers to **Q32**, above.

Once we "become aware" of them, God wants us to respond to troubles like those by caring enough to help and then doing something about them! In other words, follow Jesus's lead.

News about him spread all over…, and people brought to him all who were ill with various diseases, those suffering severe pain, the demon-possessed, those having seizures, and the paralyzed; and he healed them. (Matthew 4:24)

31 Because so many people were coming and going that (Jesus and his disciples) did not even have a chance to eat, he said to them, "Come with me by yourselves to a quiet place and get some rest." 32 So they went away by themselves in a boat to a solitary place. 33 But many who saw them leaving recognized them and ran on foot from all the towns and got there ahead of them. 34 When Jesus landed and saw a large crowd, he had compassion on them, because they were like sheep without a shepherd. So he began teaching them many things. [And later that day he fed them all.] (Mark 6:31–34)

Jesus knew very well how to say *No*; he just *didn't* very often. None of us is expected to care about and respond generously to *everyone's* needs as he did. But all of us are expected to do *something* as he did.

Like the boy seen early one morning tossing starfish into the ocean after an exceptionally stormy night. The seashore was littered with hundreds of them. A passerby commented to him that he was just one small person, so his efforts wouldn't matter much in the long run. The boy picked up another starfish, threw it into the water and replied, "It matters to that one."

Q33: Who do you know (about) with urgent needs that you can do something about, either directly or by supporting an organization that specializes in helping people like them?[70]

---

[70] By all means support the efforts of your local church, but there are also ways to help people in distress who are beyond your church's reach. For example, Samaritan's Purse offers *many* kinds of assistance in Jesus's name around the world, especially in response to disasters, but also by providing for daily needs.

CHAPTER 31
GENEROSITY WITH THE LOST

May our thinking never grow fuzzy about Jesus's main reason for leaving heaven, engaging us in person and then submitting to an exceptionally vicious death. In his own words:

The Son of Man came to seek and save the lost. (Luke 19:10)

I have come that (you) may have life, and have it to the full. (John 10:10b)

[51] I am the living bread that came down from heaven. Whoever eats this bread will live forever. This bread is my flesh, which I will give for the life of the world. ... [54] Whoever eats my flesh and drinks my blood has eternal life, and I will raise them up at the last day. (John 6:51, 54)

When everything is ready, I will come and get you, so that you will always be with me where I am. (John 14:3, NLT)

Why was Jesus so set on dying at such a young age? It must have seemed morbid and avoidable to his followers. What was his love so unflinchingly determined to rescue us from?

In the end, it was to spare us from being found guilty and condemned by God for our unrepented sins, banished from his presence and exiled to a place where his love remains forever inaccessible. Hell is unending and total darkness, utter aloneness, gnawing anguish, destitution, weeping, burning, destruction and hopelessness. It's impossible to imagine something worse.

God wants very much for no one's journey to end there. And if we feel the same way, we will do what we can to prevent it, using the most effective means we're aware of.

Many among us have adopted the saying, "Preach the gospel to everyone; use words when necessary." It makes a crucial point, because one of the most powerful arguments "outsiders" have against Christianity is Christians: "They're all just a bunch of hypocrites."

So unless they see us doing a respectable job of practicing what we preach, being less bombastic about legislating the Bible's morality on everyone, caring about *more* than our political party's priorities and working to make life better for the disadvantaged and distressed, most people will want nothing to do with us or what we believe. I know this is true.

My son recently reminded me that "people don't care what you know until they know that you care." They're sick of self-identified Christians who, in too many ways, are just like (and sometimes worse than) unbelievers. For that matter, so is Jesus.

> You are the salt of the earth. But if the salt loses its saltiness, how can it be made salty again? It is no longer good for anything, except to be thrown out and trampled by men. (Matthew 5:13)

> Keep your conscience clear. Then if people speak against you, they will be ashamed when they see what a good life you live because you belong to Christ. (1 Peter 3:16b, NLT)

Yet the saying that emphasizes preaching with words "only when necessary" is also off-balance.

> [14] How can anyone call on the Lord to save them unless they believe in him? And how can they believe in him if they have never heard about him? And how can they hear about him unless someone tells them? [15] And how will anyone go and tell them without being sent? (Romans 10:14–15, NLT)

> We are Christ's ambassadors, as though God were making his appeal through us. We implore you on Christ's behalf: Be reconciled to God. (2 Corinthians 5:20)

Words aren't everything, but they *are* necessary. And that poses a problem for us who feel uncomfortable talking about God with non-Christians. A few suggestions may help with that:

Press Less, Bless More

I used to feel guilty that I wasn't trying to convert non-Christians nearly as often or as boldly as "I was supposed to." It felt unnatural and awkward when I tried and robbed me of joy.

Then someone wise encouraged me just to love people and try to be a blessing instead of working so hard to "evangelize" them. Something about that shift immediately relaxed and liberated me. I felt less pressured to "score points" and "close the deal" and freer to be simply friendly and interested. That made talking about faith-related issues much more natural and enjoyable, and it led to many visibly-better outcomes. Nobody likes to be preached-at or pressured.

Q34: Does what you just read describe a perspective-shift you need to make? Explain.

Assist with the Next Step

³⁷ (Jesus told his disciples:) "You know the saying, 'One plants and another harvests.' And it's true. ³⁸ I sent you to harvest where you didn't plant; others had already done the work, and now you will get to gather the harvest." (John 4:37–38, NLT)

Non-Christians aren't usually converted all at once in a single, momentous event. More often it involves a lengthy process of many steps and contributions. Think of it as something like this:

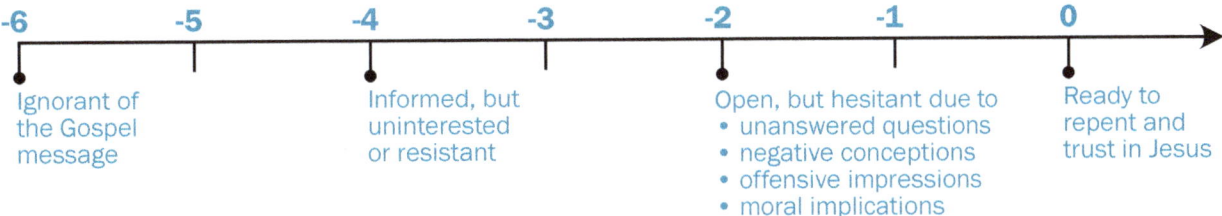

So one of the loving things we can do to help people "find Jesus" is first try to discern how far they've already progressed on their spiritual journey. Where are they at now? What do they believe and why? Where are they stuck or misinformed or ignorant? If we don't know, we need to find out. Once we understand them better, we can prayerfully consider how to help them take the next step(s) forward instead of dumping truth on them or urging them before they're ready.

We don't need to explain *everything* that people need or worry about their ultimate conclusions regarding Jesus. The part we're playing is just one among many others in their unfolding story. They are *God's* project, and how their tale ends is *mostly* between him and them.

⁵ After all, who is Apollos? Who is Paul (the Apostle)? We are only God's servants through whom you believed the Good News. Each of us did the work the Lord gave us. ⁶ I planted the seed in your hearts, and Apollos watered it, but it was God who made it grow. (1 Corinthians 3:5–6, NLT)

²⁴ A servant of the Lord must not quarrel but must be kind to everyone, be able to teach, and be patient with difficult people. ²⁵ Gently instruct those who oppose the truth. Perhaps God will change those people's hearts, and they will learn the truth. ²⁶ Then they will come to their senses and escape from the devil's trap. For they have been held captive by him to do whatever he wants. (2 Timothy 2:24–26, NLT)

Q35: When you pray, who first comes to mind that needs to take a step closer to faith in Jesus, and where (at what number) do you see them on the scale, above?

Pray for these people before you read on.

Prepare in Advance

One prospect that stabs some of us with anxiety is that we'll get a chance to talk with someone about a spiritually significant topic, then bungle it because we don't know what to say. Fear stifles our generosity by turning our attention almost entirely onto ourselves. But the reason we *feel* incompetent and ill-prepared may be that we actually *are*, and that problem can be remedied.

1. Prepare to Explain "the Gospel"

It's one thing to know the gospel well enough to make it yours, but it's another to communicate it clearly to someone else. There are many ways to do so, but an easy one is simply to recite a single verse and summarize its main points. Here's a time-tested example:

> God so loved the world that he gave his one and only Son, that whoever believes in him shall not perish but have eternal life. (John 3:16)

1. God loves and desires a close relationship with us all.

2. Our relationship with God has been ruptured/broken by our "sins" *(= disregard, disrespect and disobedience)*, and we will perish apart from him if it's not repaired.

3. God sent Jesus, his unique and only Son, to suffer the punishment our sins deserve by dying for them on our behalf/in our place.

4. Jesus overcame death and now offers us forgiveness and eternal life in a restored relationship with God.

5. We need to repent and trust ("believe") in Jesus to make us right with God.

EXERCISE: Memorize and rehearse John 3:16 along with its five summary points. An opportunity to share them is approaching in your near future.

P.S. If you want to have more than one pungent verse ready to share, another to consider is:

> The wages of sin is death, but the free gift of God is eternal life through Christ Jesus our Lord. (Romans 6:23)

You may find it helpful to memorize an expanded version of John 3:16 to make its meaning clearer without needing further explanation. Here's an example:

> "God showed his love for the entire world by sending his unique and only Son, Jesus Christ, to suffer the punishment our sins deserve, so whoever now turns to him and trusts in him will not be punished by God but receive his forgiveness and live with him forever." (John 3:16, Expanded)

2. Prepare to Discuss Common Questions and Objections

Doubting they can "defend" themselves effectively is another reason Christians may be nervous to talk about faith-related issues with doubters, especially those they know to be educated, opinionated, articulate or snarky.

You may find it reassuring to learn there are less than 20 topics that most people are likely to raise. And solid, intelligent responses are readily available for them all. Knowing them doesn't guarantee you'll be persuasive in every conversation, because some skeptics are impossible to satisfy even with sound reasoning and verifiable facts. But advance preparation can equip you to engage them much more helpfully, like learning how to do the Heimlich Maneuver before you need it.

Here's a list of the most common questions and objections I've come across over the years. Put a star next to the few that interest or concern you most and are likely to surface in a conversation. If you know of others that belong on the list, add them at the bottom.

1. Isn't everyone right in their own way? Don't we all have our own truth?

2. How can you know/prove that God exists?

3. Don't all religions believe essentially the same things?

4. Don't science and the Bible contradict each other? Can *both* be right about things like...
   - the age of the earth/universe?
   - Adam and Eve?
   - the fossil record (with dinosaurs, prehistoric humans, etc.)?
   - evolution versus creation?
   - Noah's flood?

5. What makes Christianity better/more right than other religions?

6. How could Jesus be both the Son of God and God, himself?

7. Does everyone need to believe in Jesus to get into heaven? Isn't it enough to be good?

8. What happens in the end to all the people who never hear about Jesus?

9. How could an all-loving God send people to hell?

10. How can Christianity be true/good when so many Christians are hypocrites/idiots?

11. If God is all-wise, all-loving and all-powerful, why did he create the world to have so much suffering and evil, and why doesn't he do something to fix it?

12. Why don't miracles still happen nowadays as they supposedly did in Bible times?

13. How can we completely trust the Bible when it has contradictions and errors in it?

14. What about other ancient writings that didn't make it into the Bible but should have?

15. How can we trust the Bible when it's been copied, changed and translated so many times since it was originally written (as in the "Telephone Game")?

16.

17.

Thankfully, you don't have to formulate all your own responses to these questions. Highly educated, skillful **apologists** have produced tons of written and online materials on every topic you can imagine, all of which are easily accessible. I've listed some highly-respected ones below, with asterisks next to my personal favorites.[71]

> *Apologetics* is the subject and **apologists** are the people who seek to defend the Christian faith using reason and evidence.

- **A.I.** – No kidding! Just don't automatically assume the answers you get are correct or complete without double-checking.

- ***Justin Brierly** – *Unbelievable?* on Premier Christian Radio. Great podcast with balanced debates between Christian vs. non-Christian experts on many controversial issues: unbelievable.com

- ***William Lane Craig** – The best of the best; scholarly and exact: ReasonableFaith.org

- **GotQuestions.org** – Tackles hundreds of frequently asked questions

- **Ken Ham** – Specializes in "young earth creationist" apologetics: AnswersInGenesis.org

- **Greg Koukl** – *Stand to Reason* addresses many cultural and apologetics issues: str.org

- **C. S. Lewis** – Many outstanding books including *Mere Christianity*

- **Sean McDowell** – *More Than a Carpenter; Evidence That Demands a Verdict*: SeanMcdowell.org

- ***Hugh Ross** – *Reasons to Believe* specializes in science vs. Bible issues: reasons.org

- ***Lee Strobel** – Readable approach to *many* tough questions: LeeStrobel.com

- **J. Warner Wallace** – A unique approach to apologetics: ColdCaseChristianity.com

If ever an interested or doubtful person raises a challenge and you're unsure how to respond, listen carefully to make sure you understand their point. Tell them you'll do some research and get back to them soon. Then do! But please don't wait until then to start preparing.

EXERCISE:
1. Pick one of the questions from page 217 that you find especially intriguing or challenging.
2. Ask the Spirit to guide your research and help you think through how to respond to it. Write a bullet-point summary of what you come up with in the blank space under "your" question on the pages that follow.
3. Then share your findings with a friend to see what they think. If you're in a group of others doing this exercise, write down *each other's* summaries. Better still, discuss and sharpen them if you have time. You'll end up with a good start on preparing yourself to interact with people who wonder and doubt. Someday you may even be able to save someone from choking to death.

[15] In your heart revere Christ as Lord. Always be prepared to give an answer to everyone who asks you to give the reason for the hope [and faith] that you have. But do this with gentleness and respect, [16] keeping a clear conscience, so that those who speak maliciously against your good behavior in Christ may be ashamed of their slander. (1 Peter 3:15–16)

---

[71] There are *many* others; these are just some I've become familiar with that cover a wide range of topics.

Answers to Common Questions and Objections

1. Isn't everyone right in their own way? Don't we all have our own truth?

2. How can you know/prove that God exists?

3. Don't all religions believe essentially the same things?

4. Don't science and the Bible contradict each other? Can both be right about everything?

5. What makes Christianity better/more right than other religions?

6. How could Jesus be both the Son of God and God, himself?

7. Does everyone need to believe in Jesus to get into heaven? Isn't it enough to be good?

8. What happens in the end to all the people who never hear about Jesus?

9. How could an all-loving God send people to hell?

10. How can Christianity be true/good when so many Christians are hypocrites/idiots?

11. If God is all-wise, all-loving and all-powerful, why did he create the world to have so much suffering and evil, and why doesn't he do something to fix it?

12. Why don't miracles still happen nowadays as they supposedly did in Bible times?

13. How can we completely trust the Bible when it has contradictions and errors in it?

14. What about other ancient writings that didn't make it into the Bible but should have?

15. How can we trust the Bible when it's been copied, changed and translated so many times since it was originally written (as in the "Telephone Game")?

16.

17.

3. Prepare to Tell Your Story

It will always be hard for people to dismiss the account of your encounters with God as pure fiction or delusion. It's not only rude of them to try, but you did happen to be there at the time. As an eyewitness, your testimony is at least *somewhat* credible. So think through how to share it as effectively as you can.

In Acts 26 the apostle Paul got a choice opportunity to explain to the higher-ups of his day why he was a follower of Jesus. He nailed it. Read that chapter before you continue here.

Did you notice how Paul seamlessly broke his story into three distinct parts? They provide an excellent pattern for us to follow.

PART 1 - *What you were like BEFORE you became a Christian. (How things used to be.)*

- Recount how some hardship or interaction softened your resistance and/or created a desire for more of God.

- Or talk about what you were like before you became a Christian and the negative impact it had on you and your relationships.

- Or explain how a friend's example or love was used by God to draw you to himself.

- Or describe how your study of the supportive evidence for Christianity helped you overcome your doubts or intellectual reservations.

- Or just cite some highlights of how your early years and relationships influenced you to follow Christ.

PART 2 - *Why and how you became a Christian. (What happened that changed you.)*

- Describe the event or person God used to bring you to Christ. If you can't remember one, try to pinpoint a time when you re-committed your life to Christ and tell about that. If possible, include a biblical idea or verses that became meaningful to you.

PART 3 – *What has happened to you since you became a Christian. (How things are now.)*

- What positive differences has Jesus made in your life?

Some Helpful Guidelines for Preparing Your Story

1. Jot down your memories and ideas as though you'll have no time limit for sharing them. What story would you tell about your spiritual journey if you could do so at your leisure?

2. Make it personal. You have a unique story with details that others will identify with and want to hear. Accentuate the parts that are interesting, significant and relatable.

3. Don't dwell too much on past sins. The idea is to give others a realistic picture of the person you were or the condition you were in, and why you needed God/God's forgiveness.

4. In the second segment, explain how you became a Christian clearly enough that someone listening could follow your example.

5. Avoid clichés and over-religious expressions like "sin," "repent," "blessed," "saved," "ask Jesus into your heart," etc. Speak the language of your listeners.

6. Be careful not to give the impression that "Everything is perfect now that I'm a Christian." Be real about the difference God has made and how he is still working on you.

7. Roleplay sharing your prepared testimony with one or two others (or when you next meet with your group). See if you can hit the highlights and finish it in less than five minutes without losing anything essential.

8. Fill out a Feedback sheet after you hear someone's testimony. Tell them at least one thing you appreciate and one thing they could change to make it even "better" in some way. Collect others' Feedback sheets for you and consider their suggestions.

9. You will be best prepared if you can finally distill the main points of your testimony into a two or three minute presentation. That's frequently all the time you'll have.

10. Your story is a powerful tool God can use to open people's hearts to him. Remember to also stay alert for chances to transition into more detail about the gospel message you memorized.

My Spiritual Journey

PART 1 - What I was like BEFORE I became a Christian:

PART 2 - Why and how I BECAME a Christian:

PART 3 - What's different SINCE I became a Christian:

CONCLUSION

As we wrap this up, I feel I should make a final attempt to protect you from reaching a mistaken conclusion.

We have been exploring the nature of six spiritual priorities to which every Christian should give their wholehearted attention: *knowing* God, *trusting* God, *obeying* God, *delighting in God*, *serving* God and *loving people*.

What you *might* deduce from all this is that you and I must constantly strive to excel at all six of those activities if we ever want to become "good Christians" whom God can fully love and accept.

But the truth is that we can *never* persuade him to see or respond to us like that, because he already *DOES*!

> [14] We have seen and testify that the Father has sent his Son to be the Savior of the world. [15] If anyone acknowledges that Jesus is the Son of God, God lives in them and they in God. [16] And so we know and rely on the love God has for us. God is love. (1 John 4:14–16)
>
> [32] Since (God) did not spare even his own Son but gave him up for us all, won't he also give us everything else? [33] Who dares accuse us whom God has chosen for his own? No one—for God himself has given us right standing with himself. [34] Who then will condemn us? No one—for Christ Jesus died for us and was raised to life for us, and he is sitting in the place of honor at God's right hand, pleading for us.
> [35] Can anything ever separate us from Christ's love? Does it mean he no longer loves us if we have trouble or calamity, or are persecuted, or hungry, or destitute, or in danger, or threatened with death? ... [37] No, despite all these things, overwhelming victory is ours through Christ, who loved us.
> [38] And I am convinced that nothing can ever separate us from God's love. Neither death nor life, neither angels nor demons, neither our fears for today nor our worries about tomorrow—not even the powers of hell can separate us from God's love. [39] No power in the sky above or in the earth below—indeed, nothing in all creation will ever be able to separate us from the love of God that is revealed in Christ Jesus our Lord. (Romans 8:32–35, 37–39, NLT)

Getting us to doubt this is one of the devil's most devious and effective mind games. As long as we feel uncertain about the constancy or completeness of God's love for us, as long as we think it's still possible to alienate him or exhaust his patience or diminish his affection, as long as we fear there is something wrong with us that must be fixed before we can be fully blessed or close to him, we will miss the whole point of the six spiritual priorities. And we will strain far more than necessary to express *through* them what God most wants to receive: our true and undivided *love* for him.

> *There is an order and sequence to how a mutually loving relationship with God is meant to develop.*

First he bathes us in the most beautiful and powerful force that exists: his own love. Doing that reduces—and ultimately eliminates—our innate insecurity and need to prove or improve ourselves. It also heals our injured hearts and starts filling them with an increased desire to reciprocate God's love in the six ways we've outlined.

> [18] God's pure and perfect love drives out all our fear of him and enables us to love him in return. Those who still fear God's disapproval or rejection or judgment need to go deeper in their experience of his love. [19] We can love because he first loved us. (1 John 4:18–19, Expanded Paraphrase)

So all of us who wish to love God as he desires must *frequently* revisit and re-immerse ourselves in the luxuriant, joyful and reassuring embrace of his gracious love for us. We need to focus *often* on delighting in him. Everything that is good, true, lovely and enriching is a gift from his hand. We are his and he is ours for as long as we both shall live. And it is by daily living in the light of that immutable reality that we become able to fulfill the purpose for which we were made.

So how are you doing at that?

One good way to tell is by evaluating how well you're doing at each of the six priorities. Again, they are not tasks to complete each day so you can go to sleep feeling satisfied with your performance. They are instead like the rainbow of colors created by God's pure love refracting through the prism of your heart and returning back to him. They are six beautiful ways in which your love for God can fully express itself.

Q: Which one of the six primary ways to love God most needs your attention at this time, and what can you do to improve it?

Practically everyone *can* grow to love God more and better, but most need help to know *how*. That's where you can step-in now that you've "finished" this course. If you are willing to share what you're learning with a variety of friends and groups—and if they go on to do the same— together we can raise the temperature of *many* people's love for the Lord in the days before he returns. No doubt he would love that. It's the kind of warming our poor planet desperately needs.

May he prosper all of your efforts to make it happen and share his joy with you in the process.

> [11] (I will) keep on praying for you, asking our God to enable you to live a life worthy of his call. May he give you the power to accomplish all the good things your faith prompts you to do. [12] Then the name of our Lord Jesus will be honored because of the way you live, and you will be honored along with him. This is all made possible because of the grace of our God and Lord, Jesus Christ. (2 Thessalonians 1:11–12, NLT)